HOCKEY IN SYRACUSE

SYD HOWE, CENTER/LEFT WING. Howe was inducted into the Hockey Hall of Fame in 1965. He played for Syracuse in 1931–1932 and had 21 points and 9 goals in 45 games. The hockey legend played 17 years in the NHL (1929–1946), mostly with Detroit, compiling 528 points and 237 goals in 698 games. Howe retired as the NHL's all-time point-scoring leader in 1946 with 528 points. He gained that title on March 8, 1945, when he earned his 516th point, surpassing the record held by Nels Stewart. The hall of famer won three Stanley Cups with Detroit in 1935–1936, 1936–1937, and 1942–1943.

HOCKEY IN SYRACUSE

Jim Mancuso

Published by Arcadia Publishing
Charleston SC, Chicago IL, Portsmouth NH, San Francisco CA

Printed in Great Britain

Library of Congress Catalog Card Number: 2005928687

For all general information contact Arcadia Publishing at:
Telephone 843-853-2070
Fax 843-853-0044
E-mail sales@arcadiapublishing.com
For customer service and orders:
Toll-Free 1-888-313-2665

Visit us on the internet at http://www.arcadiapublishing.com

In memory of Dave Ferguson, "The Heart of the Blazers."

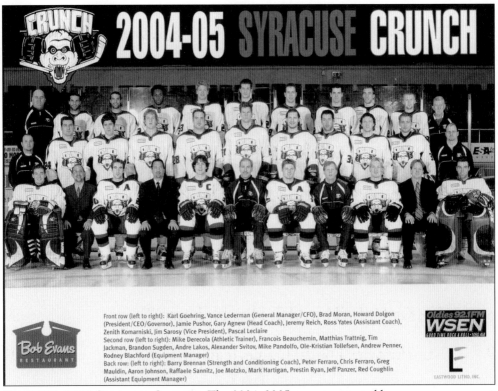

Front row (left to right): Karl Goehring, Vance Lederman (General Manager/CFO), Brad Moran, Howard Dolgon (President/CEO/Governor), Jamie Pushor, Gary Agnew (Head Coach), Jeremy Reich, Ross Yates (Assistant Coach), Zenith Komarniski, Jim Sarosy (Vice President), Pascal Leclaire
Second row (left to right): Mike Derecola (Athletic Trainer), Francois Beauchemin, Matthias Trattnig, Tim Jackman, Brandon Sugden, Andre Lakos, Alexander Svitov, Mike Pandolfo, Ole-Kristian Tollefsen, Andrew Penner, Rodney Blachford (Equipment Manager)
Back row: (left to right): Barry Brennan (Strength and Conditioning Coach), Peter Ferraro, Chris Ferraro, Greg Mauldin, Aaron Johnson, Raffaele Sannitz, Joe Motzko, Mark Hartigan, Prestin Ryan, Jeff Panzer, Red Coughlin (Assistant Equipment Manager)

THE 2004–2005 SYRACUSE CRUNCH. The 2004–2005 team is pictured here.

CONTENTS

ACKNOWLEDGMENTS

The images in this book are courtesy of Luann Horton-Murad, Ernie Fitzsimmons, the Hockey Hall of Fame in Toronto, and the Syracuse Crunch Hockey Club. Credit is due to Blazer photographer Bill Jerome and Crunch photographer Steve Cross, who were responsible for taking some of the photographs featured in this publication.

I would like to thank my imaging advisors, Edwin Duane Isenberg, Ernie Fitzsimmons, and Craig Campbell, manager of the Hockey Hall of Fame Resource Center and Archives, for their technical guidance and work on imaging the illustrations in this book.

I was helped directly through the Syracuse Crunch office by Jim Sarosy, team vice president, and Christine Porpiglio, director of public relations and advertising.

The statistics in this book were obtained from American Hockey League media guides (1951–2005), the Hockey Hall of Fame Archives in Toronto, official Eastern Hockey League press releases from P.E.M. Thompson, Ralph Slate's hockey database at www.hockeydb.com, the Society of International Hockey Research, and the second edition of *Total Hockey: The Official Encyclopedia of the National Hockey League*. Please note that official American Hockey League and Eastern Hockey League annual statistics were not broken up by team for some seasons.

Other resources used to complete this work included *The Clinton Comets: An EHL Dynasty* by Jim Mancuso and Fred Zalatan; *Before the Blade: The Story of the Buffalo Bisons* by Tim Warchocki; John Blomquist; Brian Elwell; Rex Jetter; the *Hockey News* (1947–2005); Luann Horton-Murad; the *1975 North American Hockey League Yearbook*; the *Post-Standard* of Syracuse, New York (1930–2005); the *Sporting News Hockey Guide* (1967–1981); the *1972–1973 Syracuse Blazers First Annual Yearbook*; the *1973–1974 Syracuse Blazers Second Annual Yearbook*; and Fred Zalatan.

A special thanks to my mother, Joan Mancuso, who was a ticket sales representative at the Utica Memorial Auditorium during the 1970s and got me in free to see the Syracuse Blazers make hockey history.

INTRODUCTION

Syracuse has a rich and storied professional hockey history that spans several eras of minor-league hockey. The Syracuse Stars were one of the earliest professional hockey teams in the United States. The Stars, who existed from 1930–1931 through 1939–1940, had a formal affiliation with the Toronto Maple Leafs from 1932–1933 to 1938–1939. Several of the Syracuse players assigned by Toronto—Bob Davidson, Gordie Drillon, Reg Hamilton, Rudolph "Bingo" Kampman, Pete Langelle, and Nick Metz—helped build the Maple Leafs' Stanley Cup dynasty of the 1940s. Hall of famers Gordie Drillon and Dave "Sweeney" Schriner started their professional hockey careers in the Salt City. Syd Howe, another hall of famer who played with the Stars, went on to lead the Detroit Red Wings to three Stanley Cups.

The early 1950s saw Eddie Shore's Warriors skate at the new state-of-the-art Onondaga War Memorial. Salt City hockey fans had the opportunity to see hall of famer Keith "Bingo" Allen and hockey legends Bep Guidolin and Joseph "Bronco" Horvath. For three seasons (1951–1954), area fans witnessed perhaps the highest caliber of play in American Hockey League (AHL) history during the National Hockey League's (NHL) "original six" era.

The Chicago Black Hawks put their Eastern Professional Hockey League (EPHL) outfit in Syracuse in 1962–1963. The Syracuse Braves became the first United States–based team in the history of the EPHL. Hall of famer Phil Esposito and NHL great Roger Crozier began their first full seasons of professional hockey in Syracuse. The EPHL was a young and fast league composed of several of the NHL's top prospects.

The Syracuse Blazers (1967–1977) were one of the greatest franchises ever to hit the ice in minor-league professional hockey. They had a humble beginning, as most expansion teams do, but evolved into a record-breaking dynasty. The Blazers won three playoff championships: the Eastern Hockey League's (EHL) Walker Cup in 1972–1973 and the North American Hockey League's (NAHL) Lockhart Cup in 1973–1974 and 1976–1977. Syracuse's 22-game winning streak (set in 1973–1974) and 85-game unbeaten streak at home (1971–1972 to 1973–1974) are still professional hockey records. In 1972–1973, the Salt City sextet was the first professional hockey team ever to reach 60 wins and 130 points. Blazer Ray Adduono set professional hockey records for points in a season (165) and assists in a season (122) in 1971–1972. Adduono broke his own point record in 1972–1973 with 170 points.

In 1974–1975, Syracuse fans experienced two professional teams in one season. The Syracuse Eagles were born when the most successful franchise in AHL history, the Cleveland/Jacksonville

Barons, was purchased by a group headed by Bill Charles and moved to the Salt City. Syracuse fans had the opportunity to watch the AHL Eagles or the EHL Blazers, both at the War Memorial.

Two more teams entertained Salt City hockey fans around the turn of the next decade. The Syracuse Firebirds (AHL), brought to town from Philadelphia in 1979–1980 by the owner of Mrs. Paul's Kitchens, gave fans a chance to see top prospects from the Pittsburgh Penguins and Quebec Nordiques organizations skate at the War Memorial. In 1980–1981, the Syracuse Hornets (EHL) became the first team since the old Syracuse Stars (International-American Hockey League) to schedule all of their home games at the State Fairgrounds Coliseum.

Hockey returned in 1994–1995 with the Syracuse Crunch, the most successful Salt City hockey team in terms of longevity and fan base. From 1994–1995 through 2004–2005, the Crunch have drawn over 200,000 fans each season at the War Memorial; a grand total of almost 2.5 million supporters have passed through the turnstiles. The team has also experienced success on the ice, winning a regular-season conference championship, capturing a division title, and participating in the Calder Cup playoffs in 7 of its 11 seasons.

In 1997–1998, the AHL All-Star Game and Skills Competition were hosted by Syracuse due to the franchise's success. Mike Peca (two-time Frank J. Selke Trophy winner), Jamie Pushor (two-time Stanley Cup winner), Jassen Cullimore (Stanley Cup winner), and Scott Walker (10-year NHL veteran) are just a few of the NHL stars who played for Syracuse. The Crunch have provided area fans with a high caliber of hockey and have established themselves as one of the top sporting attractions in the Salt City as well as in central New York.

ONE

THE STARS
PIONEERS OF PROFESSIONAL HOCKEY IN SYRACUSE

Professional hockey began in Syracuse in 1930–1931, when the Syracuse Stars became members of the International Hockey League (IHL). The Syracuse Professional Hockey club, a locally based organization with Nicholas M. Peters as its president, purchased the IHL's Hamilton Tigers franchise and transferred it to the Salt City. The IHL was known as the Canadian Professional Hockey League (CPHL) from 1926–1927 to 1928–1929, but changed its name for the 1929–1930 campaign because a substantial number of its teams were now below the border.

The Stars did not shine in their first season, finishing in last place out of seven teams with a 9-34-5 record. The Stars' first coach, Percy LeSueur, was replaced midseason by Frank Foyston. Both LeSueur and Foyston were future hall of famers. Two bright spots were forwards Jack Markle and Pete Palangio, who both finished the season in the league's top 10 in points and goals. Markle finished fifth in points (38) and ninth in goals (18), while Palangio ranked seventh in points (32) and sixth in goals (20).

The Stars improved slightly in 1931–1932 with new coach Mickey Roach, but they missed the playoffs, finishing in sixth place out of seven with a record of 16-23-9. Markle again made the top 10 in points (tied for fifth with 33) and goals (fifth with 20), while Frank Waite led the league in assists (26) and was tied for fifth in points (33). Syd Howe, who went on to a Hockey Hall of Fame career, played for the Stars in 1931–1932.

In 1932–1933, the Stars formed a formal affiliation with the Toronto Maple Leafs that lasted until the 1938–1939 season. The Leafs' farmhands gave the Stars a boost as the locals iced their first winning season (23-15-6), placing third out of six teams, and made the playoffs for the first time. The top four teams in the standings competed for the Teddy Oke Trophy, named after one of the early pioneers of hockey in the 20th century, in a six-game round-robin playoff, with each team playing two games against each opponent. The Stars tied for second in the round-robin with a 2-3-1 record. Syracuse scored the most goals in the IHL regular season (136) and had three players among the league's top-10 point scorers: Scott "Flash" Martin (fifth with 38), Earl Miller (eighth with 34), and Stewart Adams (tied for ninth with 33).

Syracuse's offensive prowess continued in 1933–1934, as the team once again lead the league in goals scored (114). It also placed four players in the IHL's top-10 point scorers: Earl Miller (first with 40), Al Huggins (third with 37), Jack Markle (fourth with 36), and future Hockey Hall of Fame inductee David "Sweeney" Schriner (tied for ninth with 28). However, the club barely made the playoffs with its 19-21-4 record, finishing fourth out of six teams. The IHL again had a four-team, six-game round-robin playoff. Just after the playoffs began, Stars captain Earl Miller replaced Mickey Roach as coach of the team for the remainder of the postseason. Syracuse finished tied for third in the round-robin with a 2-4 record.

Eddie Powers became the new coach of the Stars in 1934–1935. For the third consecutive season, the "Twinklers" led the league in offense (128 goals), but they finished with a .500 record (20-20-4) in third place out of six. Markle led the IHL in scoring (43 points), while Ken Doraty and Al Huggins (29 points) were both tied for ninth. The top four teams qualified for the playoffs, but a new series format was adopted. The Stars were pitted against the first-place Detroit Olympics in a best-of-three semifinal. Syracuse was swept in two games.

The IHL had an eight-team, two-division format in 1935–1936. Syracuse was in the Eastern Division. The Stars had a high turnover that year, with eight new players on the squad. Seven of the newcomers were youngsters who had been handpicked by Maple Leafs general manager Conn Smythe and assigned to the locals. Smythe's hockey expertise was evident as the Stars captured the Eastern Division title with a 26-19-3 record. For the first time, Syracuse had the most points in the standings (55), tied with the Western Division winners, the Detroit Olympics. The "Twinks" scored an IHL record 167 goals, shattering the previous record set by the Windsor Bulldogs (141) in 1930–1931. It was the fourth consecutive season that the Stars led the league in goals. Markle (27), rookie George Parsons (20), rookie Jack Shill (20), and Eddie Convey (20) all placed in the league's top 10 for goals scored. Goaltender Phil Stein had a goals against average (GAA) of only 2.26 in 40 games. That season, the two division champions faced each other in an opening round best-of-five series, with the winner given a direct berth into the finals. Syracuse faced Detroit and was swept in three games.

DAVID "SWEENEY" SCHRINER, LEFT WING. Schriner, inducted into the Hockey Hall of Fame in 1962, started his professional hockey career in Syracuse in 1933–1934 while on loan for the season from the New York Americans (NHL). He had 28 points and 17 goals in 44 games with the Stars. Sweeney's NHL career spanned from 1934 to 1946 with the Americans and the Maple Leafs. He scored 201 goals and tallied 405 points in 484 games, and he won two Stanley Cups with Toronto in 1941–1942 and 1944–1945. The hall of famer also won two Art Ross Trophies, given to the NHL's leading scorer, in 1935–1936 and 1936–1937. He was given the Calder Trophy for NHL rookie of the year in 1934–1935.

BENNY GRANT, GOALIE. Grant was between the pipes with the Stars from 1931 through 1934. He had an impressive 2.45 GAA in 1931–1932 and a 2.70 GAA in 1932–1933 for Syracuse. The goaltender appeared in six NHL seasons between 1928 and 1944 with Toronto, the Americans, and Boston, earning a 3.75 GAA and a 17-26-4 record in 50 games. He was in net for five games with the 1931–1932 Stanley Cup–winning Maple Leafs.

EARL MILLER, LEFT WING. Miller played two seasons for the Stars, from 1932 through 1934, scoring 40 goals and garnering 74 points in 87 games. Miller was promoted from Syracuse team captain to coach during part of the 1933–1934 playoffs. Prior to coming to the Salt City, he played five seasons in the NHL, from 1927 through 1932, with Chicago and Toronto, including 15 games with the 1931–1932 Stanley Cup–winning Maple Leafs.

CHARLIE SANDS, CENTER/RIGHT WING. In 1932–1933, Sands had 15 points and 10 goals in 37 games with the Stars. A veteran of 12 NHL seasons (1932 through 1944) with Toronto, Boston, the Canadiens, and the Rangers, he compiled 208 points and 99 goals in 427 games. Sands won a Stanley Cup with the Bruins in 1938–1939.

PETE PALANGIO, LEFT WING. Palangio was a member of the Stars during the club's first two seasons (1930 to 1932), scoring 30 goals and 47 points in 84 games. He played five seasons in the NHL between 1926 and 1938 with the Canadiens, Detroit, and Chicago, including a stint with the Stanley Cup–winning Black Hawks in 1937–1938. Palangio won three American Hockey Association (AHA) playoff championships in 1934–1935, 1935–1936, and 1937–1938 with St. Louis.

LOUIS TRUDEL, LEFT WING. Trudel played only five games with the Stars in 1933–1934. The left winger spent eight NHL seasons (1933–1941) with Chicago and the Canadiens, collecting 118 points and 49 goals in 306 games. Trudel played for the Stanley Cup–winning Chicago teams in 1933–1934 and 1937–1938 and the Calder Cup–winning Cleveland AHL teams in 1944–1945 and 1947–1948.

BILL THOMS, CENTER. Thoms played two seasons in Syracuse (1931–1933), earning 20 points and 9 goals in 32 games. He played 13 years in the NHL (1932–1945) with Toronto, Boston, and Chicago, compiling 341 points and 135 goals in 548 games.

LAUDAS "DUKE" DUTKOWSKI, DEFENSE.
Duke skated for the Stars during the
1933–1934 season. The defenseman spent
five seasons in the NHL between 1926 and
1934 with the Black Hawks, the Americans,
and the Rangers. He earned 46 points and
16 goals in 200 games. Dutkowski also
played major-league hockey in the Western
Canada Hockey League from 1921 to 1925
and in the Western Hockey League in the
1925–1926 season.

HAROLD "HOWL" DARRAGH, LEFT WING.
In two seasons with the Stars (1932–1934),
Darragh produced 39 points and 16 goals in
68 games. He played eight seasons in the NHL
(1925–1933) with Pittsburgh, Philadelphia,
Boston, and Toronto. Howl had 117 points and
68 goals in 308 NHL games and won a Stanley
Cup with the Maple Leafs in 1931–1932.

THE 1934–1935 STARS. The Stars, from left to right, include Dave Downie, Ken Doraty, Ronnie Martin, Jack Markle, Dud James, Helge Bostrom, Scotty Martin, Bob Davidson, Nick Metz, Phil Stein, Archie Wilcox, Bill Gill, and Reg Hamilton. The team finished in third place with a 20-20-4 record and made the playoffs. Syracuse was eliminated in a best-of-three semifinal series, falling to the Detroit Olympics in two games.

JIMMY "SAILOR" HERBERTS, CENTER/RIGHT WING. An original Boston Bruin in 1924–1925, Sailor had a two-game stint with the Stars during the 1932–1933 season. He had a six-year career in the NHL (1924–1930) with Boston, Toronto, and Detroit, compiling 112 points and 83 goals in 206 games.

STEWART "STEW" ADAMS, LEFT WING. In 1932–1933, Stew spent part of the season with the Stars and with parent club Toronto (NHL). He had 33 points and 11 goals in 36 games with Syracuse. Prior to coming to the Salt City, Adams played three seasons in the NHL with Chicago (1929–1932). He won an AHA playoff championship with Minneapolis in 1927–1928.

AL MURRAY, DEFENSE. Murray played during the 1933–1934 season with Syracuse. He had 28 penalty minutes (PIM) and one point in nine games. The defenseman spent seven seasons in the NHL with the New York Americans (1933–1940), totaling 14 points and 5 goals in 271 games. Prior to coming to the Stars, he won back-to-back Teddy Oke Trophies with Buffalo in 1931–1932 and 1932–1933.

JOE MILLER, GOALIE. Miller played his last season of professional hockey with Syracuse. He had a 2.55 GAA in 20 games with the Stars in 1931–1932. Prior to arriving in Syracuse, the goaltender played four seasons in the NHL (1927–1931) with the Americans, the Rangers, Pittsburgh, and Philadelphia. He had a 2.92 GAA and a record of 24-87-16 in 127 NHL games.

HARRY "YIP" FOSTER, DEFENSE. In 1939–1940, Foster had 13 points in 55 games with Syracuse. He spent four seasons in the NHL between 1929 and 1935, playing with the Rangers, Boston, and Detroit. Yip won a Calder Cup with Cleveland in the International-American Hockey League (IAHL) in 1938–1939, a Teddy Oke Trophy with Detroit (IHL) in 1935–1936, and two Fontaine Cups in the Canadian-American Hockey League (CAHL), one with Springfield in 1927–1928 and one with Boston in 1932–1933.

TWO

THE STARS
CALDER CUP CHAMPIONS

The first major change in the setup of minor-league hockey came in 1936–1937, when the International Hockey League (IHL) and the Canadian-American Hockey League (CAHL) combined to form the International-American Hockey League (IAHL). The IAHL had an eight-team, two-division format, and Syracuse was placed in the Western Division. The IAHL became known as the American Hockey League (AHL) in 1940–1941.

The new league brought new fortune for the Stars, as they won their first-ever playoff championship. Syracuse captured the Calder Cup (named after NHL president Frank Calder, who was instrumental in the formation of the IAHL) after defeating the Eastern Division champion Philadelphia Ramblers three games to one in the playoff finals. The Stars defeated the Pittsburgh Hornets three games to two in the semifinals. During the regular season, under coach Eddie Powers, the Stars won the Western Division title with a 27-16-5 record and scored a league-leading 173 goals. Jack Markle won the IAHL's first scoring title with 60 points. Eddie Convey and Norm Mann placed fourth (49 points) and seventh (41 points) in league scoring, respectively. Phil Stein was credited with all 27 team wins in goal, leading the IAHL. He played in every one of his team's 48 games, again leading the IAHL, and secured a 2.72 GAA. Hall of famer Gordie Drillon, assigned by Toronto, played with the Stars during that first IAHL season.

In 1937–1938, the Stars, whose lineup had few changes from the previous season, almost successfully defended their championship. The "Twinks" swept Pittsburgh in the first round and swept the Cleveland Barons in the semifinals, both in best-of-three series. They fell short of a repeat, however, losing in the finals against the Providence Reds three games to one. The club achieved its third consecutive winning record (21-20-7) in 1937–1938, finishing third in the Western Division. Syracuse also led their league in goals scored (142) for the sixth year in a row. Markle and Convey placed first and second in league scoring with 54 and 52 points, respectively. Defenseman Chuck Shannon was selected to the IAHL's first team all-stars, while Markle and Convey made the second team.

In 1938–1939, the Stars achieved a fourth-straight winning season with a record of 26-19-9 and a second-place finish in the Western Division. The postseason saw a first-round exit to Providence, two games to one. The Syracuse offense was led by Murray Armstrong, ranked fourth in IAHL scoring with 54 points, and Norm Locking, ranked eighth in IAHL scoring with 50 points. Defenseman Jack Church was named to the IAHL first team all-stars, while Coach Eddie Powers tied for first team honors.

Several changes occurred entering the 1939–1940 season. After having been affiliated with Toronto for the last seven seasons, the club now operated independently, and new player/coach Jack Markle had to build an entirely new club practically from scratch. The lack of Maple Leaf farmhands hampered the Stars' play, and the team suffered its first losing season in six years (20-27-9), finishing in last place in the Western Division and out of the playoffs. Locking, named a first team IAHL all-star, earned 63 points to become the "Twinklers" third scoring champion in the four-year existence of the IAHL. Max Bennett placed fourth in league scoring with 56 points.

Shortly after the 1939–1940 season ended, Louis and Marvin Jacobs of Buffalo, owners and operators of the Stars franchise, announced that they were seeking local ownership to take over the team. The Jacobs brothers, who had taken over the Stars in 1937–1938, wanted to sell the club because they were losing money. Also a factor in the owners' withdrawal was Louis Jacobs's partnership in the new Buffalo IAHL franchise, scheduled to play in 1940–1941 at the newly built Buffalo Memorial Auditorium.

The absence of the Toronto (NHL) affiliation during the 1939–1940 season was the primary reason for the Stars' financial woes. It was more expensive for the Jacobs to operate their team as an independent outfit than it had been when the club had a working agreement with the Maple Leafs. There was also a deficiency in patronage during the 1939–1940 campaign, which was also attributed to the lack of NHL affiliation, due to having a weak team on the ice. There was not much time for another group of owners to step up, because the lease option on the Coliseum was due to expire just months after the Jacobs made their announcement. No new group bought the team, the time elapsed, and the team folded. The Syracuse Stars compiled a 207-214-61 (.493) regular-season record during their 10-year history.

GORDIE DRILLON, RIGHT WING. Drillon was inducted into the Hockey Hall of Fame in 1975. He played five games with Syracuse during the 1936–1937 season and had five points and two goals before being called up to Toronto (NHL). In his seven-year NHL career (1936–1943) with Toronto and Montreal, the hockey legend tallied 294 points and 155 goals in 311 games. The hall of famer won a Stanley Cup with Toronto in 1941–1942. He also won an Art Ross Trophy for NHL leading scorer and a Lady Byng Trophy for NHL most sportsmanlike player in 1937–1938.

HIGH SCORERS. The Stars were known as a high-scoring team during their 10-year existence (1930–1940). In every one of their seasons, they had more than one player place in their league's top 10 points scored category, including five scoring champions. The "Spanglers" also led their league in goals scored in six seasons, from 1932–1933 to 1937–1938. Syracuse scored an all-time IHL record of 167 goals in 1935–1936.

BILL THOMSON, CENTER/RIGHT WING. Thomson played his first professional season with the Stars in 1937–1938. He also played parts of the 1938–1939 and 1939–1940 seasons in the Salt City. He had two stints in the NHL with Detroit (1938–1939 and 1943–1944). The right winger won an AHA playoff championship with Omaha in 1941–1942 and played for Calder Cup–winning Hershey (AHL) in 1946–1947.

JACK MARKLE, RIGHT WING. Markle was the only player to skate in all 10 of the Stars' seasons. He is the team's all-time leader in points (420), goals (178), assists (242), and games played (449). Markle is second all-time in points (267) in CPHL/IHL history (1926–1936). He also ranks second in goals (137) and second in assists (130) in CPHL/IHL history.

RUDOLPH "BINGO" KAMPMAN, DEFENSE. In 1937–1938, Kampman played his only season with Syracuse, appearing in just 12 games and earning three points and two goals. Bingo played five seasons in the NHL with Toronto (1937–1942), including the 1941–1942 Stanley Cup–winning team. He had 44 points and 14 goals in 189 NHL games.

LORNE CARR, RIGHT WING. In 1933–1934, he had 12 points and 8 goals in 18 games for Syracuse. Carr played 13 years in the NHL (1933–1946) with the Rangers, the Americans, and Toronto. He compiled 426 points and 204 goals in 580 NHL games and won two Stanley Cups with Toronto (1941–1942 and 1944–1945). Carr, Dave Schriner, and Gus Bodnar formed the Maple Leafs' "Bacon Line."

JACK SHILL, CENTER. Shill played for the Stars in 1935–1936 and had 40 points, 20 goals, and 82 PIM in 46 games. He played 160 games in six NHL seasons (1933–1939) with Toronto, Boston, the Americans, and Chicago. Shill won a Stanley Cup with the Black Hawks in 1937–1938, a Calder Cup with Providence (IAHL) in 1939–1940, and a Fontaine Cup with Boston (CAHL) in 1934–1935.

NICK METZ, LEFT WING. In 1934–1935, he scored 13 goals and tallied 26 points in 26 games with Syracuse. Metz went on to a 12-year career in the NHL with Toronto (1934–1942 and 1944–1948), winning four Stanley Cups (1941–1942, 1944–1945, 1946–1947, and 1947–1948). He had 250 points and 131 goals in 518 NHL games. Metz, Gordie Drillon, and Syl Apps formed the "Big Line" that skated for the Maple Leafs.

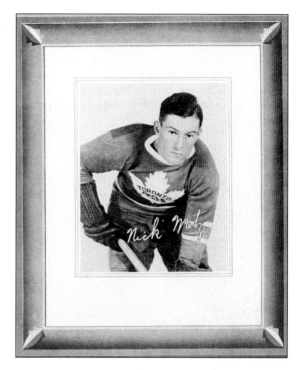

NORM MANN, RIGHT WING/CENTER. Mann spent three seasons with the Stars (1935–1937 and 1938–1939), tallying 103 points and 36 goals in 137 games. The Maple Leaf assignee was briefly in the NHL with Toronto for parts of three seasons between 1935 and 1941. Mann was with Calder Cup–winning Providence (IAHL) in 1939–1940.

A Toronto Affiliate. The Syracuse Stars adopted the patriotic uniform style of the New York Americans (NHL), but they were never an affiliate of the Big Apple club. The Stars were a farm team of the Toronto Maple Leafs (NHL) for seven seasons (1932–1933 to 1938–1939). The working agreement with the Leafs appeared to correlate with the rise and fall of the Salt City franchise. The Stars began to experience success on the ice at the beginning of the Toronto affiliation, but they had one of their worst seasons and then folded after the relationship was severed. Many players assigned to Syracuse by Maple Leafs general manager Conn Smythe went on to stellar NHL careers. Star players that were under contract with Toronto included Stewart Adams, Murray Armstrong, Mickey Blake, Frank "Buzz" Boll, Jack Church, Ken Doraty, Gordie Drillon, Benny Grant, William "Flash" Hollett, Rudolph "Bingo" Kampman, Norm Mann, Nick Metz, Earl Miller, Charlie Sands, Chuck Shannon, Jack Shill, and Bill Thoms.

MICKEY DROUILLARD, CENTER.
Drouillard played with Syracuse in
1931–1932 and had 14 points and 9 goals.
After skating with the Stars, Drouillard
spent two more seasons in the IHL with
Windsor and Detroit. The center also
played in the AHA (1934–1937) with
Oklahoma City, Minneapolis, and Tulsa,
and in the IAHL/AHL (1936–1942)
with Pittsburgh, Providence, Hershey,
Springfield, Buffalo, and Philadelphia.

WILLIAM "FLASH" HOLLETT, DEFENSE.
Hollett played for the Stars in 1932–1933
and 1935–1936, earning five points in
23 games. Flash was in the NHL for 13
seasons (1933–1946) with Toronto, Ottawa,
Boston, and Detroit. The defenseman
had 313 points and 132 goals in 562 NHL
games. He won two Stanley Cups with
Boston in 1938–1939 and 1940–1941.

BILL TOUHEY, LEFT WING. Touhey split the 1934–1935 season between Syracuse and Windsor (IHL). Prior to coming to the Stars, he played seven NHL seasons (1927–1934) with the Maroons, Ottawa, and Boston, garnering 105 points and 65 goals in 280 games.

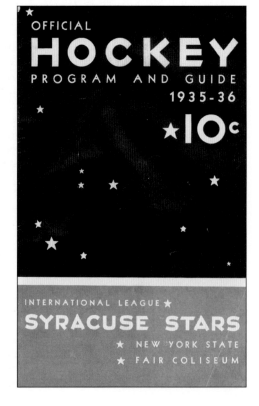

A 1935–1936 STARS PROGRAM. This program is from a game versus the Cleveland Falcons on January 31, 1936, during the last season of the International Hockey League (IHL). The IHL merged with the Canadian-American Hockey League (CAHL) in 1936–1937 to form the International-American Hockey League (IAHL). The IAHL changed its name to the American Hockey League (AHL) prior to the 1940–1941 season.

THREE

THE WARRIORS
EDDIE SHORE'S TEAM

The American Hockey League Board of Governors, with thoughts of expanding the league, persuaded Eddie Shore to move his Springfield Indians (AHL) to the brand-new, state-of-the-art Onondaga War Memorial in 1951–1952. A contest was held to name the team, and the club was renamed the Syracuse Warriors.

Eleven years had gone by without professional hockey in Syracuse. The Springfield Indians, who had been owned by Eddie Shore since the 1939–1940 season, were one of the oldest teams in minor professional hockey. The Indians were original members of the Canadian-American Hockey League in 1926–1927. In 1951–1952, Springfield not only lost its team to Syracuse but also became the Salt City's farm team over the next three seasons. The new Springfield Indians, also owned and managed by Shore, competed in the EAHL (known as the EHL from 1954 through 1973) from 1951 to 1953. After the EAHL suspended operations, the team competed in the Quebec Hockey League (QHL) in 1953–1954.

The AHL had nine teams and a two-division alignment in 1951–1952. The Warriors, coached by Frank Beisler, were in the Eastern Division. Shore described his team as "young and fast"; the average player age was just over 22 years. The Warriors, who operated independently of an NHL affiliation, did not fare well in their first season, going 25-42-1 and finishing in last place in their four-team division. Kelly Burnett, who was sixth in AHL scoring that season, led the team with 68 points and was tied with Harry Pidhirny for the most goals on the team (25). Gordon Bell anchored the goaltending duties, finishing seventh in the AHL in GAA (3.87). Bell was credited with 24 of the team's 25 victories and appeared in 63 of his team's games. Other notable players during the Warriors' first season were future hall of famer Keith "Bingo" Allen and Bronco Horvath.

After two teams dropped out, the AHL changed its league format to a single division composed of seven teams for the 1952–1953 season. Syracuse broke even at 31-31-2, which was good enough for third place and a playoff spot. The Cleveland Barons knocked the Warriors out in the first round of the playoffs, three games to one. Burnett, named a second team AHL all-star at center, again had the best offensive performance for the locals (76 points), this time placing fourth in AHL scoring. Allen tied for a second team defensive position on the AHL all-star team. Pidhirny led the team in goals with 34. Bell finished third in AHL goaltending with a 3.13 GAA, led the league in shutouts with six, appeared in all of his team's 64 games, and was credited with all 31 wins. Bep Guidolin, the youngest player ever to play a regular-season game in the NHL, skated for the Warriors in 1952–1953.

The AHL shrank to six teams in 1953–1954. There was a high turnover on the Warriors that season—there were nine new players on the 18-man squad. The lack of experience on the team, along with the fact that it was one of three AHL teams without an NHL working agreement, may have contributed to Syracuse finishing in last place with a 24-42-4 record. Horvath led the offense with 60 points, and Pidhirny led the team in goals with 31. Bell finished fifth in league goaltending with a 3.59 GAA, earning 21 of his team's 24 wins. Pidhirny tied the all-time AHL record for goals in a game with six against Providence on November 21, 1953. That record still stands today.

Shortly after the 1953–1954 season ended, the Warriors' stay in Syracuse was threatened when Shore had a disagreement with War Memorial officials over scheduling home games for the 1954–1955 season. Shore lost four choice Saturday night dates, and the alternate days offered in their place proved to be unacceptable to the league. The AHL told Shore that unless he could get as many Saturdays as past seasons, the league might be forced to find him a new city. Two months passed, and the conflict had not been resolved. In a league meeting in mid-June, the AHL revoked the Warrior franchise because the club could not obtain the War Memorial on enough dates to play a complete home-and-home schedule. It was learned that the four Saturday nights the hockey team had lost were given to a boxing promoter for nationally televised fight programs, which paid about six times the rental fee of a hockey game.

Shore, whose team incurred losses of considerably more than $100,000 in its three seasons in Syracuse, had planned on keeping the Warriors in the Salt City. Instead he had to move his team back to Springfield. The Warriors had an overall regular-season record of 80-115-7 (.413) from 1951–1954.

EDDIE SHORE, OWNER AND GENERAL MANAGER. The "Edmonton Express" was responsible for bringing professional hockey back to Syracuse when he relocated his Springfield Indians to the Salt City for three seasons (1951–1954). Shore, one of the greatest defenseman ever to play the game, bought the Springfield club in 1939–1940 and owned the team until 1975–1976, with the exception of 1942–1946, when Springfield suspended operations due to the U.S. Quartermaster Corps using its arena during the war. As a player in 14 NHL seasons (1926–1940), Shore was the only defenseman to win the Hart Trophy (given to the NHL's MVP) four times. He anchored two Stanley Cup–winning teams for Boston (1928–1929 and 1938–1939) and was named to the NHL all-star team eight times, including seven first team selections. In 1970, the NHL awarded Shore with the Lester Patrick Trophy for "outstanding service to hockey in the United States." He was inducted into the Hockey Hall of Fame in 1947.

KEITH ALLEN

KEITH "BINGO" ALLEN, DEFENSE. Allen was inducted into the Hockey Hall of Fame as a builder in 1992. He holds the Warrior record for most games played (178) and had 63 points, 11 goals, and 62 PIM during his three seasons with Syracuse (1951–1954). The defenseman played for Stanley Cup–winning teams in Detroit in 1953–1954 and 1954–1955, and he won a Calder Cup with Buffalo (AHL) in 1942–1943. He was the first coach in Philadelphia Flyers history, from 1967–1969, and he built back-to-back Stanley Cup champions in 1973–1974 and 1974–1975 when he was promoted to general manager of the Flyers. Bingo has the distinction of being the only coach ever to lead a team to a Calder Cup championship during its first two seasons of existence, which he accomplished in Maine in 1977–1978 and 1978–1979. He also coached Seattle to a President's Cup championship in 1958–1959 in the Western Hockey League (WHL).

JOSEPH "BRONCO" HORVATH, CENTER.
Horvath is second all-time in points (167), assists (115), and PIM (154) in Warriors history. The center had 52 goals in 148 games from 1951 to 1954 and led the locals in scoring in 1953–1954 with 60 points. Bronco played nine seasons in the NHL (1955–1963 and 1967–1968), registering 141 goals and 326 points. He won three Calder Cups with Rochester (AHL) in 1964–1965, 1965–1966, and 1967–1968.

BRONCO HORVATH

BEP GUIDOLIN, LEFT WING.
In November 1942, Guidolin became the youngest player to ever play a regular-season NHL game; he was 16 years and 11 months old. He played nine seasons in the NHL (1942–1944 and 1945–1952), earning 107 goals and 278 points in 519 games. In 1952–1953, he had nine points and eight assists in 23 games with Syracuse. Guidolin later coached in the NHL and the World Hockey Association (WHA).

HARRY PIDHIRNY

HARRY PIDHIRNY, CENTER. Pidhirny is the all-time leading goal scorer of the Warriors with 90 goals. From 1951 to 1954, the center appeared in 170 games with Syracuse, third on the Warriors' all-time list. Pidhirny ranks among the all-time leaders in AHL history: sixth in goals (376), seventh in points (829), and third in games played (1,071). He resurfaced as the Blazers' first general manager and coach in 1967–1968. Pidhirny played with Boston (NHL) in 1957–1958.

KELLY BURNETT, CENTER. Burnett is the Warriors' all-time leader in points (181) and assists (125). He led the Warriors in scoring during their first two seasons, scoring 68 points in 1951–1952 and 76 points in 1952–1953. After playing with Syracuse, he spent seven seasons with Montreal (1954–1961) in both the QHL and the EPHL. The center also had a stint in the NHL with the Rangers in 1952–1953.

BILLY GOODEN, LEFT WING. Gooden is second all-time in goals (57) and fourth all-time in points (130) for the Warriors. He also netted 57 goals in 166 games during his three seasons with Syracuse (1951–1954). He played for the Rangers (NHL) from 1942 to 1944 and had a stint with the Calder Cup–winning Providence (AHL) in 1955–1956.

BILL GOODEN

DOUG MCMURDY

DOUG MCMURDY, CENTER. In his only season with the Warriors in 1951–1952, McMurdy had 35 points, 22 goals, and 22 PIM in 48 games. McMurdy also spent seven other seasons in the AHL with Pittsburgh (1945–1946) and Springfield (1948–1951 and 1954–1957). He played for Syracuse's farm club in Springfield (EAHL and QHL) from 1951 to 1954 and was the team's player/coach from 1952 to 1954.

GEORGE FORD, FORWARD. Ford played in three seasons with Syracuse (1951–1954). His best season was in 1951–1952, when he had 27 points, 11 goals, and 25 PIM in 51 games. Ford spent most of his career in the WHL (1954–1964) with five different teams. The forward also played in the AHL with Baltimore, Springfield, and Pittsburgh between 1950 and 1963.

DON ASHBEE, LEFT WING. In 1952–1953 with Syracuse, Ashbee had 27 points and 7 goals in 42 games. Prior to coming to Syracuse, Ashbee played in the AHL with Buffalo (1949–1951) and Indianapolis (1951–1952). He later played with Cleveland's (AHL) 1953–1954 Calder Cup–winning team.

RALPH HOSKING, DEFENSE. Hosking split the 1951–1952 season between Syracuse and Halifax of the Maritime Major Hockey League (MMHL). He had 11 points in 40 games with the Warriors. Prior to coming to the Salt City, he played four seasons in the AHL with Springfield (1947–1951).

RALPH HOSKING

Gordon Tottle

GORDON TOTTLE, DEFENSE. Tottle holds the Warriors' all-time record for PIM with 187. In his three seasons in Syracuse (1951–1954), he had 52 points and 45 assists in 147 games. Tottle played seven additional seasons in the AHL with Springfield (1947–1951 and 1954–1957), four seasons in the EHL with Charlotte (1958–1962), and spent time in the IHL, QHL, WHL, and the United States Hockey League (USHL).

DANNY SUMMERS, DEFENSE. In his two seasons with the Warriors (1951–1952 and 1953–1954), Summers had 34 points and 28 assists in 107 games. He earned a Calder Cup with Providence (AHL) in 1948–1949, a President's Cup with Winnipeg (WHL) in 1955–1956, and a Turner Cup with St. Paul (IHL) in 1959–1960 and 1960–1961.

ARMAND LEMIEUX, LEFT WING. Lemieux played two seasons with the Warriors (1951–1953), garnering 103 points and 47 goals in 124 games. Prior to his arrival in Syracuse, Lemieux spent seven seasons in the AHL between 1943 and 1951, playing with Springfield, Pittsburgh, and Providence.

ERIC POGUE, RIGHT WING. Pogue was a Warrior for two seasons (1952–1954). The 1953–1954 campaign was his best performance in the Salt City: He had 45 points, 21 goals, and 68 PIM in just 36 games. The right winger spent part of the 1950–1951 season with Calder Cup champion Cleveland (AHL).

LEO CURICK

LEO CURIK, CENTER. In three seasons with the Warriors (1951–1954), Curik produced 66 points, 36 goals, and 56 PIM in 123 games. Prior to coming to Syracuse, he played two seasons in the AHL with Springfield (1948–1949 and 1950–1951).

ED HARRISON, CENTER. In 1952–1953, his only season with the Warriors, Harrison played for five teams in four leagues. Besides Syracuse, he also spent time with Quebec in the Quebec Senior Hockey League (QSHL), St. Louis in the AHL, Vancouver in the WHL, and Washington in the EAHL. Harrison was a veteran of four NHL seasons (1947–1951) with Boston and New York.

SAMMY CASANATO, RIGHT WING. In two seasons with Syracuse (1951–1953), he garnered 67 points, 20 goals, and 230 PIM in 130 games. Casanato holds the Warriors' single-season penalty minute record with 144, which he set in 1951–1952. Casanato played with Springfield (AHL) from 1949 to 1951 and also spent a season in both the USHL (1948–1949) with Fort Worth and the Pacific Coast Hockey League (1947–1948) with San Diego and Tacoma.

MIKE NARDUZZI, LEFT WING. Narduzzi had 76 points, 38 goals, and 40 PIM in 127 games during his two seasons with Syracuse (1951–1952 and 1953–1954). The left winger was with the Warriors' farm club in Springfield (EAHL) in 1952–1953 and for part of the 1953–1954 season, when the team was a member of the QHL. He also played in the AHL with Philadelphia and Springfield across five seasons (1946–1950 and 1954–1955).

MIKE NARDUZZI

JOHN ASHLEY, DEFENSE. Ashley played only part of the 1952–1953 season with Syracuse after arriving from Pittsburgh, but he took part in the Warriors' Calder Cup playoff run. Ashley also played with Pittsburgh (AHL) in two other seasons (1950–1952) and was a member of the 1951–1952 Calder Cup–winning team.

FRANK BEISLER, COACH. Beisler piloted the Warriors in all three of their seasons (1951–1954). He had previously coached in the AHL with Buffalo (1945–1947), Washington (1948–1949), and New Haven (1950–1951), winning a Calder Cup with Buffalo in 1945–1946. As a player, the defenseman skated for three Calder Cup–winning teams in Buffalo (1942–1943, 1943–1944, and 1945–1946).

A 1951–1952 WARRIORS PROGRAM. Coming to the Salt City was not the only move that Eddie Shore made with his Springfield club. During World War II, the Indians' home rink was used by the U.S. Quartermaster Corps from 1942–1946. Shore negotiated a deal with former Syracuse Stars owner Louis Jacobs, the owner of the Buffalo Bisons (AHL), which allowed Shore to transfer his players to Buffalo and take control of the franchise.

FOUR

THE BRAVES
THE BLACK HAWKS CHOOSE SYRACUSE

The Syracuse Braves became the first United States–based team in the four-year history of the Eastern Professional Hockey League when the Chicago Black Hawks transferred their EPHL affiliate to the Salt City in 1962–1963. The Black Hawks' EPHL club had been the Sault Ste. Marie Thunderbirds from 1959 to 1962. The EPHL was organized in 1959–1960 with six teams, and until the 1962–1963 season, it had consisted only of teams located in the provinces of Ontario and Quebec.

The loop had only four teams in Syracuse's first season: the Braves and three original members, Hull-Ottawa, Kingston, and Sudbury. Chicago (NHL) owned and operated the Braves franchise. Over one-third of the players on the Syracuse roster had played for the Sault Ste. Marie Thunderbirds during the previous season. Due to the lack of teams in the circuit, the EPHL played a partial interlocking schedule with the International Hockey League, a loop formed in the Midwest in 1945–1946.

The Braves were based at the Onondaga War Memorial and were scheduled to play a 72-game season with 36 home dates. Walter "Gus" Kyle was named coach. Several outstanding players hit the ice for the Syracuse Braves: future hall of famer Phil Esposito, Roger Crozier, Alain "Boom Boom" Caron, and Murray Hall.

The team's stay in Syracuse was a short one—it left town on New Year's Eve and headed to St. Louis for the remainder of the schedule. The Syracuse Braves played only 30 games, posting a dismal 6-18-6 (.300) record. The biggest single reason for the move was the poor attendance at home games. In 16 home appearances at the War Memorial, the Braves drew an average of just under 700 fans per game. In the preseason, it had been determined that the club needed to draw an average of 3,000 spectators per game in order to be financially successful. Chicago Black Hawks general manager Tommy Ivan told the Associated Press, "We have a lot of good young prospects on the Syracuse club, and I didn't think it was doing any good to be playing before such skimpy home turnouts."

The Syracuse/St. Louis Braves finished in last place with a 26-37-9 record. The Braves were the only team in the league to miss the playoffs; the second-place and third-place teams faced off to meet the first-place team in the finals for the Foley Trophy championship. Despite not making the postseason, the team boasted several standout players. Phil Esposito finished in the

EPHL's top 10 in all three offensive categories: sixth in points with 90, fifth in goals with 36, and tied for fourth in assists with 54. Boom Boom Caron established a new EPHL record for goals in a season with 61. Murray Hall led the league in assists with 69 and tied for ninth in goals with 29. Merve Kuryluk finished ninth in scoring with 75 points and tied for sixth in assists with 53. Goaltender Roger Crozier played in a league-high 70 games and posted a league-leading 4,200 minutes between the pipes. Crozier was credited with a 26-35-9 record and a 4.27 GAA.

The 1962–1963 season was the last for the EPHL. One month after the loop folded, a new league, the Central Professional Hockey League (CPHL), was formed out of teams from the EPHL and IHL. The CPHL began play in 1963–1964. It was known as the Central Hockey League (CHL) from 1968–1984.

PHIL ESPOSITO, CENTER. Esposito started his first full season of professional hockey with the Syracuse Braves. In 1962–1963, he was sixth in the EPHL in points (90), fifth in goals (36), and tied for fourth in assists (54). He was enshrined in the Hockey Hall of Fame in 1984. When the hockey legend retired from the NHL in 1981, his 717 goals and 1,590 points were second all-time, surpassed only by Gordie Howe's totals, and his 873 assists were third all-time. Esposito earned two Stanley Cups with Boston in 1969–1970 and 1971–1972. The hall of famer won five Art Ross Trophies as NHL leading scorer (1968–1969, 1970–1971, 1971–1972, 1972–1973, and 1973–1974) and two Hart Trophies as NHL MVP (1968–1969 and 1973–1974). He was named to the NHL all-star team eight times, including six times to the first team. Esposito served as general manager and, briefly, as coach of the New York Rangers between 1986 and 1989. He also helped land an NHL expansion team in Tampa Bay and served as the Lightning's general manager from 1992 to 1998.

ROGER CROZIER, GOALIE. Crozier played his first full professional season with the Syracuse/St. Louis Braves before embarking on a stellar NHL career. He played 14 NHL seasons, compiling a 3.04 GAA and a 206-197-70 record in 518 games with Detroit, Buffalo, and Washington. In 1962–1963, Crozier led the EPHL in games played (70) and minutes played (4,200) while recording a 26-35-9 record with Syracuse/St. Louis.

ALAIN "BOOM BOOM" CARON, RIGHT WING. Caron scored 732 goals professionally. He set the all-time EPHL record for goals in a season (61) with the Braves in 1962–1963. Caron also set the all-time single-season goal mark (77) in CHL history in 1963–1964, and he tied a professional hockey record for goals in a season (78) while playing in the NAHL (1975–1976). He also played with the Syracuse Blazers (1974–1975).

MURRAY HALL, RIGHT WING. Hall was the leading scorer of the Braves with 98 points. He led the EPHL in assists (69) and tied for ninth in goals (29) in 1962–1963. He played nine seasons in the NHL (1961–1968 and 1970–1972) with Chicago, Detroit, Minnesota, and Vancouver, compiling 83 points and 35 goals in 164 games. Hall won two Avco World Trophies (1973–1974 and 1974–1975) with the Houston Aeros (WHA).

GEORGE "DUKE" HARRIS, RIGHT WING. Harris was fifth in scoring with the Braves with 59 points. He also netted 28 goals. Harris had stints in the NHL with Minnesota and Toronto during the 1967–1968 season. The Duke had 100 points and 53 goals in three seasons in the WHA (1972–1975) with Houston and Chicago. He also won Calder Cups (AHL) in Pittsburgh (1966–1967) and Rochester (1967–1968).

DENNIS KASSIAN, LEFT WING. Kassian registered 40 points and 20 goals in 32 games with the Braves. He played five seasons in the AHL (1965–1970) with Buffalo and Pittsburgh, winning a Calder Cup in Buffalo (1969–1970). The left winger also spent time in the CPHL (1963–1965) and the WHL between 1960 and 1972 with various teams. He made it to the major leagues with the Alberta Oilers (WHA) in 1972–1973.

MILAN MARCETTA, CENTER. Marcetta had 13 points and 9 goals in 20 games with Syracuse/St. Louis. He played in the WHL for 13 seasons, winning Patrick Cups with Victoria in 1965–1966 and Denver in 1971–1972. (The WHL playoff trophy was called the President's Cup prior to 1960–1961.) The center shares the all-time WHL record for goals in a game with five. Marcetta skated in the NHL with Minnesota (1967–1969) and Toronto (1966–1967).

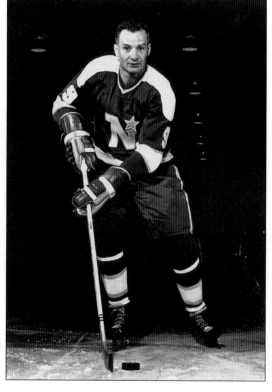

NICK POLANO, DEFENSE. In 1962–1963, Polano led the Braves and placed second in the EPHL in PIM (152). He tallied 33 points in 71 games for Syracuse/St. Louis. The defenseman went on to coach two seasons in the NHL with Detroit (1982–1984). Polano led Erie (EHL) to three consecutive Mitchell Cups from 1978–1979 to 1980–1981. The EHL was known as the North Eastern Hockey League (NEHL) in 1978–1979.

HEC LALANDE, CENTER. Lalande tallied 30 points and 6 goals in 26 games for Syracuse/St. Louis. The center had four seasons of NHL experience (1953–1954 and 1955–1958) with Chicago and Detroit, tallying 60 points and 21 goals in 151 games. He played seven years in the AHL (1954–1955 and 1956–1962), winning two Calder Cups in Hershey (1957–1958 and 1958–1959). He also won a Walker Cup championship with Clinton (EHL) in 1963–1964.

FIVE

THE BLAZERS
WALKER CUP CHAMPIONS

The Eastern Hockey League, which originated in December 1933, expanded to Syracuse in 1967–1968. The new Syracuse entry, nicknamed the Blazers, established a working agreement with the Boston Bruins that lasted through 1971–1972. The team was based at the Onondaga War Memorial.

The Blazers did not experience much success in their first season; they had problems from the start, both financially and on the ice. The team had a 12-57-3 record and finished in last place in the six-team North Division. Crowd size was poor, and the team also failed to win any road games. Syracuse had the distinction of using six coaches during its inaugural campaign. Former Syracuse Warrior Harry Pidhirny, Dave Cusson, Wayne Caufield, Carlo Longarini and Ray Adduono (co-coaches), and Clobie Collins piloted the team. Despite the team's lack of success, there were some memorable season highlights. Ray Adduono was named North Division Rookie of the Year and placed second in EHL scoring with 146 points. Tim McCormick set all-time EHL records for points in a game (12) and assists in a game (7) versus the Jersey Devils on February 24, 1968.

EHL legend Ray Crew took over the coaching reigns as a player/coach in 1968–1969 in the hopes of taking the expansion team to the next level. But the Blazers lacked talent and took a step backward, posting a 9-59-4 record. Crowds continued to be very small.

Crew was back in 1969–1970 but strictly as a bench coach. The team gained respectability as it began to win consistently at home and occasionally on the road. Attendance continued to be dismal, however, and the club was on the brink of folding midseason before Bill Charles assumed general manager duties. With Charles operating the team, the Blazers not only finished out the season (23-37-14 record in fourth place) but they made the playoffs. In the postseason, the locals lost four straight to the Clinton Comets. Adduono won his first EHL scoring crown with 134 points.

In 1970–1971, behind Coach Phil Watson, the Blazers had their first winning season, posting a 36-30-8 record and finishing second in the North Division. Watson was named an EHL North team all-star. The Blazers also won their first postseason game against the Johnstown Jets, but they went on to lose the series in six games. Adduono finished 10th in EHL scoring with 101 points. Home attendance reached over the 100,000 mark for the first time in a season.

Syracuse won the EHL's North Division title in 1971–1972 in what was a tight race for most of the season. The Blazers, who clinched first place in the final week of the schedule, were awarded the Atlantic City Boardwalk Trophy for winning the North Division. New coach Ron Ingram led the team to a 38-27-10 finish and a trip to the Walker Cup finals. The Blazers won their first playoff series against the New Haven Blades in a quarterfinal that went seven games. They grounded the Johnstown Jets in the semifinals, four games to two, before bowing to the Charlotte Checkers in four straight games. Adduono shattered professional hockey records for points in a season with 165 and assists in a season with 122. LaRose was second in EHL scoring with 129 points and set an all-time Blazer record for goals in a season with 67. Adduono, Ingram, and LaRose were named to the North Division All-Star Team. Attendance skyrocketed, reaching over 200,000.

In 1972–1973, Syracuse not only reached its ultimate goal of winning the Walker Cup, but also had one of the greatest seasons in the history of minor-league hockey. With a 63-9-4 record, good for 130 points, Syracuse became the first professional hockey team to crack the 60-win and 130-point marks. Syracuse won 21 straight regular-season games, setting a professional hockey record, and went the entire season at home without a loss (36-0-2). Some home games were played at the State Fairgrounds Coliseum. The team's 453 goals were an all-time EHL record. There were six 100-point scorers, led by Adduono, whose 170 points broke his own professional hockey record. Yves Belanger (2.39 GAA) and Joe Junkin (2.83 GAA) finished one-and-two in EHL goaltending. Five of the six EHL first team all-stars were Blazers. The Boardwalk Trophy stayed in Syracuse as the team won a second consecutive North Division title. The road to the Walker Cup championship included two four-game sweeps over the Rhode Island Eagles and Cape Cod Cubs and a series win in the finals against the Roanoke Valley Rebels in six games.

It was announced on May 1, 1973, that the EHL was dissolving into two new leagues, the North American Hockey League (NAHL) and the Southern Hockey League (SHL). Syracuse, along with some of the cities in the EHL's North and Central Divisions, formed the nucleus of the NAHL.

BLAKE BALL, DEFENSE. Ball was one of the most intimidating players ever to take the ice. He played three seasons with Syracuse (1971–1973 and 1975–1976), totaling 64 points and 301 PIM in 109 games. The defenseman was a key ingredient in the Blazers' Walker Cup team (1972–1973). Ball also played for the Syracuse Eagles (AHL) and made it to the big leagues during the Cleveland Crusaders' (WHA) 1972–1973 playoff run. The EHL legend appeared in the 1977 movie *Slap Shot* as character Gilmore Tuttle, who played on the fictitious Syracuse Bulldogs. Ball was cast in the role because of his aggressiveness on the ice. He led the EHL in PIM from 1965–1966 to 1968–1969 and ultimately became second all-time in PIM (2,290) in the history of the EHL, which was in existence from 1933 to 1973.

RAY ADDUONO, CENTER. Adduono is the greatest playmaker and most prolific scorer ever to play in the EHL, ranking 18th all-time in points (716) and ninth all-time in assists (501) after only five seasons. Adduono topped 100 points in all five of his EHL seasons (1967–1968 and 1969–1973). In 1971–1972, he set professional records for points (165) and assists (122) in a season. He broke his own all-time point record in 1972–1973 with 170. Assigned to Syracuse by Boston (NHL) in 1967–1968, he was voted EHL North Division Rookie of the Year in 1967–1968 and was a North team all-star in 1971–1972 and a first team all-star in 1972–1973. Adduono set all-time Blazer records for points (743), goals (222), assists (521), and games played (379) during his six years with Syracuse (1967–1968 and 1969–1974). He played five seasons in the WHA (1973–1978), registering 197 points in 221 games.

DOUG FERGUSON, CENTER. Doug Ferguson played five seasons with the Blazers (1968–1973), winning a Walker Cup in 1972–1973. He is third all-time in assists and fourth all-time in points and games played in Blazer history. He also ranks fifth all-time in goals and third all-time in PIM in club history. He is the twin brother of Blazer teammate Dave Ferguson. Doug Ferguson also skated for the Syracuse Eagles (AHL).

DAVE FERGUSON, RIGHT WING.
Dave Ferguson is the Blazers' all-time PIM king (873). The right winger played four seasons with the Blazers (1969–1970 and 1971–1974) and was a member of the 1972–1973 Walker Cup and 1973–1974 Lockhart Cup championship teams. Ferguson ranks fifth on the Blazers' all-time lists in points (279) and assists (175) and is sixth all-time in goals (104). He is tied for fifth all-time in games played (233) in club history. He also skated for the Eagles (AHL).

MIKE MORTON, RIGHT WING.
Dubbed "The Mighty Mite," Mike played four seasons in the Salt City (1970–1974). Morton is second all-time in points (345) and assists (209) in Blazer history and third all-time in goals (136) and games played (298). He led the Blazers in points (95) and tied for the team lead in goals (44) in 1973–1974. Morton also played for the Syracuse Eagles (AHL).

55

BILLY ORR, DEFENSE. Orr produced 131 points and 35 goals in 138 games during two seasons with the Blazers (1971–1973). The defenseman was a member of the 1972–1973 Walker Cup team. Orr moved up to the WHA with the Toronto Toros (1973–1974), earning 12 points and 16 PIM in 46 games. He also played for the Syracuse Eagles (AHL).

LEE INGLIS, LEFT WING. Inglis played five seasons for Syracuse (1968–1970, 1971–1972, and 1973–1975) over a seven-year stretch, interrupted by playing two seasons in Holland. Inglis places high on several Blazer all-time lists: third in points (318), second in goals (137), fourth in assists (181), and second in games played (303). He skated with Claude "Gomer" Chartre and Dave Ferguson on the Blazers' famed "Construction Line" in 1973–1974.

GORDIE GALLANT, CENTER.
Gallant racked up 231 PIM and 51 points in 63 games for the 1972–1973 championship Blazers. He went on to play four years in the WHA (1973–1977) with Minnesota, Quebec, and Birmingham, compiling 849 PIM and 90 points in 273 games. Gallant joined Syracuse under contract with Cleveland (WHA). In 1979–1980, he won an Adams Cup with Salt Lake City (CHL).

RAY SCHULTZ, DEFENSE.
Schultz holds the Blazer's all-time single-season penalty minute record with 341 PIM, set in 1971–1972, and he ranks fourth on the club's all-time list in that category with 520 PIM. The defenseman played two seasons with Syracuse (1971–1973) and was a member of the 1972–1973 Walker Cup championship team. His older brother is the legendary Dave "The Hammer" Schultz. Ray Schultz appeared in the movie *Slap Shot*.

AL RYCROFT, LEFT WING. Rycroft generated 100 points and 50 goals in just 48 games for the 1972–1973 Walker Cup champions. Rycroft was assigned to Syracuse by the Cleveland Crusaders (WHA) and was called up briefly to the parent club in 1972–1973. He also played for the Syracuse Eagles (AHL).

NORM COURNOYER, CENTER. Assigned to Syracuse by Cleveland (WHA), Cournoyer had 118 points (placing sixth in EHL scoring) and 47 goals in 76 games for the 1972–1973 champion Blazers. He played two seasons in the WHA (1973–1974 and 1976–1977) with Cleveland and San Diego, earning 11 points in 32 games. The center played for Pacific Hockey League (PHL) champion San Francisco in 1977–1978 and is the brother of Montreal (NHL) great Yvan Cournoyer.

YVES BELANGER, GOALIE. Assigned to Syracuse by Cleveland (WHA) in 1972–1973, Belanger was awarded the George L. Davis Jr. Trophy as the EHL's leading goaltender (2.39 GAA) during that championship season with the Blazers. He played six seasons in the NHL (1974–1980) with St. Louis, Atlanta, and Boston, compiling a 3.76 GAA in 78 games.

GARY GRESDAL, DEFENSE. In 1971–1972, Gresdal, playing with Jersey (EHL), set the professional hockey single-season PIM mark at the time with 392. (Richmond's [AHL] Dave Schultz tied Gresdal for the record that season.) In 1972–1973, Gresdal had 256 PIM and 39 points in 52 games for the Walker Cup–winning Blazers. Gresdal played with the Syracuse Eagles (AHL) and had a stint in the WHA with the Quebec Nordiques (1975–1976).

BRIAN ELWELL, RIGHT WING. Elwell played four seasons with Syracuse (1968–1972) and had 225 points and 95 goals in 233 games. A Blazer assistant coach during the 1973–1974 season, Elwell was promoted to general manager of the Blazers in 1974–1975. In 1994, the Blazer fan favorite helped bring professional hockey back to Syracuse. Elwell also served as a radio personality for the Syracuse Crunch.

PAUL LaROSE, FORWARD. LaRose scored the fourth most goals (120) in Blazer history and holds the team's all-time record for goals in a season with 67 (set in 1971–1972). In his three seasons with the Blazers (1970–1973), he tallied 227 points in 164 games. LaRose ranks second all-time in NAHL history in points (427), goals (179), assists (248), and games played (287).

JOE JUNKIN, GOALIE. Junkin was named an EHL first team all-star in 1972–1973 after earning a GAA of 2.83 in Syracuse's Walker Cup championship season. He helped the Blazers attain the NAHL's Governors Cup (given to the regular-season champions) in 1974–1975 with a 3.65 GAA. The goaltender played in the NHL with Boston (1968–1969) and in the WHA with New York/Jersey (1973–1974) and San Diego (1974–1975).

BARRY BROOKS, FORWARD. Brooks was a member of Syracuse's 1972–1973 record-breaking team. Assigned to the Blazers by Cleveland (WHA), he had 79 points and 41 goals in 75 games that championship season. He also skated in the Salt City with the Eagles and had 21 points in 70 games.

BILL CHARLES, OWNER AND GENERAL MANAGER. Bill Charles holds the Atlantic City Boardwalk Trophy in 1972–1973. Charles was general manager of the Blazers from the middle of the 1969–1970 season until the end of the 1972–1973 campaign. He built a championship franchise. In 1971–1972, Charles was named Minor League Hockey Executive of the Year by the *Hockey News*. He spearheaded a group that brought the AHL back to Syracuse in 1974–1975.

RON INGRAM, GENERAL MANAGER AND COACH. Ingram coached the Blazers for three seasons (1971–1974). He won two playoff championships and two regular-season championships in 1972–1973 and 1973–1974 and took the Blazers to the playoff finals in each of the seasons that he piloted the team. Ingram had an amazing regular-season winning percentage of .729 (155-52-18) and a postseason winning percentage of .723 (34-13) with Syracuse.

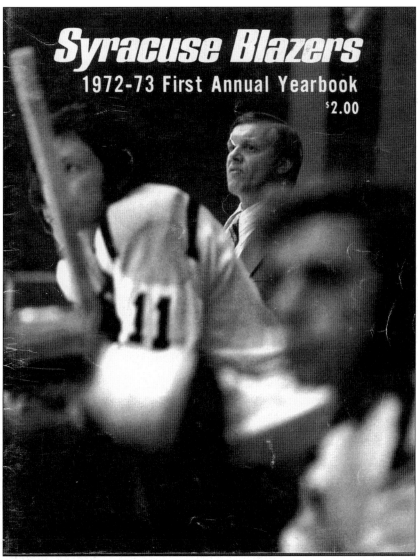

Syracuse Blazers
1972-73 First Annual Yearbook
$2.00

THE 1972–1973 BLAZERS. The *1972–1973 Syracuse Blazers First Annual Yearbook* was the first publication of its kind for the team. The full-color cover featured Coach Ron Ingram, Al Rycroft (No. 11), and Brian Elwell (far right) behind the Blazer bench. The magazine contained a brief history of the team and was marketed in the *Hockey News*. In 1972–1973, the Blazers had one of the greatest seasons in minor-league hockey history. The team won the EHL's Walker Cup championship and established professional hockey records for regular-season wins (63), points in a season (130), and consecutive regular-season wins (21). The club established an all-time EHL record for goals scored during the regular season (453) and had six 100-point scorers: Ray Adduono (170), Dave Ferguson (120), Norm Cournoyer (118), Mike Morton (105), Doug Ferguson (100), and Al Rycroft (100). The 63-9-4 club had a 12-2 playoff record and went the entire season unbeaten at home (36-0-2). Five out of the six players on the EHL first all-star team were Blazers: Joe Junkin, Billy Orr, Norm Schmitz, Adduono, and Rycroft. Yves Belanger (2.39 GAA), who was named a second team all-star, and Joe Junkin (2.83 GAA) were the top two goaltenders in the EHL that season. The team was affiliated with the Cleveland Crusaders (WHA).

LES CALDER, RIGHT WING. The right winger skated with the Blazers for parts of three seasons (1971–1974) and had 11 points in 17 games. Calder was an assistant coach for Syracuse in 1973–1974. He played a total of 11 EHL seasons with Knoxville, Long Island, and Syracuse. In 546 EHL games, Calder had 580 points (28th all-time in EHL history) and 281 goals (18th all-time in EHL history).

NORM SCHMITZ, DEFENSE. Schmitz registered 48 points and 15 goals in 69 games for the 1972–1973 Walker Cup team and was an EHL first team all-star that season. He spent five previous seasons in the EHL (1967–1972) with Long Island and New Haven. The defenseman won an Adams Cup with Oklahoma City (CPHL) in 1965–1966.

SIX

THE BLAZERS
LOCKHART CUP CHAMPIONS

The North American Hockey League (NAHL) began play in the fall of 1973. The Blazers established an affiliation with the WHA's New York Golden Blades (who became the Jersey Knights midseason). Ron Ingram now doubled as general manager and coach.

The Blazers continued their winning ways in the new league. Syracuse won the league's regular season by 19 points and went on to win the playoff championship, capturing the Governors Cup and the Thomas Lockhart Cup (named after the longtime EHL president), respectively. They went 54-16-4 in the regular season and set a professional hockey record with a 22-game winning streak, breaking their own 1972–1973 record. The season also saw the Blazers extend their unbeaten streak at home to 85 games, a professional hockey record. The locals were 14-2 in the postseason, including a four-game sweep of the Long Island Cougars in the finals. Bob "Butch" Barber, a first team all-star, was voted NAHL MVP and Outstanding Defenseman. The club had six all-star selections on the NAHL's first and second teams. Bob Costas was the play-by-play man for Syracuse in 1973–1974.

In 1974–1975, the Blazers earned a 46-25-3 record and captured a second Governors Cup with their third consecutive regular-season title. The team was led by Coach Garry Peters and general manager Brian Elwell. The Blazers, who now shared the War Memorial with the Eagles (AHL), were affiliated with the WHA's San Diego Mariners (formerly the Jersey Knights) and Michigan Stags (who became the Baltimore Blades midseason). First team all-star center Bobby Jones led the league in scoring with 114 points, while Brian Perry placed sixth in the NAHL with 88 points. Other first team all-stars included defensemen Reg Krezanski and Gary Sittler. Sittler led the league in PIM with 262. Second team all-star Bob Blanchet established NAHL all-time single-season records for GAA with 2.93 and shutouts with four. Syracuse had a first-round bye in the playoffs but lost in the semifinals in seven games to the Johnstown Jets.

The league expanded to a 10-team, two-division format for the 1975–1976 season. The Blazers occupied the East Division. Dan Belisle became general manager and coach, and the club was affiliated with the Cleveland Crusaders (WHA). Syracuse, which placed second in the division with a record of 38-33-3, missed a first-place finish for the only time in five seasons. Belisle was voted NAHL Coach of the Year and named a first team all-star, as was goalie Jacques Caron (3.10 GAA), the NAHL's second leading goaltender and former Syracuse Eagle. Defenseman

Reg Krezanski was tied for a second team slot. Doug Brindley placed 10th in league scoring with 101 points. Syracuse beat the Mohawk Valley Comets three games to one in the quarterfinals. In the semifinals, the locals were swept in four games by the Beauce Jaros.

The NAHL was down to eight teams and one division for the 1976 1977 season. The Blazers' parent team was the WHA's Minnesota Fighting Saints (formerly the Cleveland Crusaders). Syracuse earned a 48-22-3 record and won its third Governors Cup, capturing its fourth regular-season title in five years. Among the NAHL's top scorers were Bernie Johnston, who placed fifth with 124 points, Tom Milani, who placed sixth with 121 points, and Jim Cowell, who placed eighth with 110 points. NAHL Rookie of the Year Milani was named a first team all-star, as were NAHL Best Defenseman Jim Marsh and NAHL Coach of the Year Dan Belisle. Defenseman Sittler was named a second team all-star. The Blazers received a first-round bye in the playoffs for their first-place finish, and they lost only one game on the way to their second Lockhart Cup championship. They beat the Erie Blades in the semifinals four games to one and then swept the Maine Nordiques in the finals.

At the end of the fourth NAHL campaign, the Blazers were put up for sale due to large monetary losses. There were no buyers. Team officials wanted to suspend operations for one season, but the NAHL terminated the franchise. In mid-August, the NAHL granted a franchise to a group headed by Joseph Carlone, who was part-owner, general manager, and coach of the new Syracuse Condors. But the Condors franchise was revoked just two weeks later because of a lack of financial backing. A last-ditch effort by the league to financially back a new Utica team was voted down in a meeting in late September, and NAHL representatives from the only four teams ready to operate voted to dissolve the circuit.

The Blazers were the most successful team ever to take the ice in the Salt City. They won three playoff championships, captured five first-place finishes (including four regular-season league championships), and had seven winning seasons (1970–1971 to 1976–1977) in their 10-year existence. Their regular-season won/lost percentage of .535 makes them the only winning franchise (367-315-56) in Syracuse hockey history.

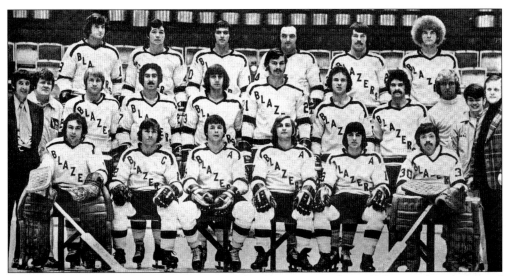

THE 1973–1974 BLAZERS. In 1973–1974, the Blazers were the NAHL's regular-season and playoff champions. The club had a 54-16-4 regular-season record and a 14-2 mark in the playoffs. In the postseason, the Blazers had a 6-1 record in the NAHL's round-robin playoff qualifier. They beat the Johnstown Jets in the semifinals four games to one and swept the Long Island Cougars in four games to win the championship. Syracuse established two minor-league hockey records in 1973–1974 that still stand today: a 22-game winning streak and an amazing 85-game unbeaten streak at home that dated back to the 1971–1972 season. There were six NAHL all-stars on the roster: Gary Kurt, Ted Ouimet, Butch Barber, and Claude Chartre were named to the first team, and Lee Inglis and Ron Ingram were named to the second team. Among the NAHL's top-10 scorers were Mike Morton, who was 9th with 94 points, and Jamie Kennedy, who was 10th with 93 points. Kurt (2.92 GAA) and Ouimet (3.03 GAA) finished first and second in league goaltending.

MIKE SMITH, DEFENSE. Smith played five seasons for the Blazers (1972–1977) and skated on three championship teams (1972–1973, 1973–1974, and 1976–1977). In his four NAHL years with Syracuse, he had 68 points, 31 goals, and 159 PIM in 142 games. The defenseman had 28 points and 106 PIM in 58 EHL games in 1972–1973 with Syracuse and Long Island.

CLAUDE "GOMER" CHARTRE, CENTER. Gomer was assigned to the Blazers by the New York Golden Blades (WHA) in 1973–1974. In his only season with Syracuse, he had 84 points and 43 goals in 47 games and was named a NAHL first team all-star. Chartre had stints in the WHA with the New York Raiders (1972–1973), the New York Golden Blades/Jersey Knights (1973–1974), and the Michigan Stags/Baltimore Blades (1974–1975).

THE BLAZERS' DEFENSE. The Blazers defend their goal against the Broome Dusters in a NAHL contest during the 1973–1974 season. The Syracuse players pictured are, from left to right, Gary Sittler (No. 4), Reg Krezanski (No. 24), Bart Buetow (No. 10), and Gary Kurt (in goal).

BOB "BUTCH" BARBER, DEFENSE. Butch spent only one season with the Blazers (1973–1974), but he had a major impact on the club. Barber, who was named to the NAHL first team all-stars, helped lead the team to a Lockhart Cup championship as the NAHL's MVP and Outstanding Defenseman. He also set an all-time NAHL single-season record for assists by a defenseman (66) in 1973–1974.

GARY SITTLER, DEFENSE. Sittler is second all-time in PIM in Blazer history. The defenseman played four seasons for Syracuse (1972–1975 and 1976–1977) and was a member of three Blazer championship teams (1972–1973, 1973–1974, and 1976–1977). Sittler is the all-time NAHL penalty minute king with 760 PIM. He was named a second team NAHL all-star in 1976–1977. His brother is NHL veteran Darryl Sittler.

TED OUIMET, GOALIE.
Ouimet played two seasons with the Blazers (1971–1972 and 1973–1974), helping the team win the Lockhart Cup in 1973–1974. He led the NAHL in wins that championship season with a 24-7-3 log, including a personal 14-game winning streak. A NAHL first team all-star in 1973–1974, he had a 2.97 GAA. Ouimet played in the NHL with St. Louis in 1968–1969.

REG KREZANSKI, DEFENSE.
Krezanski played three seasons for the Blazers (1973–1976), registering 109 points and 306 PIM in 157 games. He was a member of the 1973–1974 Lockhart Cup team. The defenseman had a stint in the WHA with San Diego in 1974–1975. Krezanski skated for Turner Cup champion Dayton in 1969–1970. He also spent three seasons (1970–1973) in the EHL with Long Island and Cape Cod.

BILLY GOLDTHORPE, LEFT WING. Goldthorpe was one of the most notorious villains in hockey history, receiving a lifetime ban from playing in the SHL. At one time, he was prohibited from setting foot in any NAHL arena. He was also refused the opportunity to try out for a team in the EHL by the league commissioner. Goldthorpe's reputation made it to Hollywood—he was portrayed in the 1977 movie *Slap Shot* as the character Ogie Ogilthorpe. Nicknamed "Harpo," Goldthorpe was a member of the Blazers' 1973–1974 championship team. He also played for the Blazers in 1974–1975. He had 285 PIM in 57 games during his two seasons with Syracuse. Goldthorpe played in the WHA (1973–1976) with Minnesota, Michigan/Baltimore, Denver/Ottawa, and San Diego, compiling 87 PIM in 33 WHA games. "Goldy" also played for the Syracuse Eagles (AHL).

GARY KURT, GOALIE. Assigned by New York (WHA), Kurt helped Syracuse capture a Lockhart Cup championship in 1973–1974 with a 2.94 GAA in 24 games. He played five seasons in the WHA (1972–1977) with New York, Jersey, and Phoenix, and he had a 72-86-7 record with a 4.17 GAA in 176 games. Kurt won the Harry "Hap" Holmes Award in the AHL for fewest goals against in 1970–1971 with Cleveland.

RUSS GILLOW, GOALIE. Gillow played a key backup role between the pipes for Syracuse during the 1973–1974 and 1974–1975 seasons, when he earned a 2.84 GAA and a 1.86 GAA, respectively. He spent four years in the WHA (1972–1976), posting a 3.50 GAA in 109 games. In 1972–1973, his GAA of 2.88 was second in the WHA. The goaltender shares the all-time record for the most shutouts (12) in the history of the CHL.

JAMIE KENNEDY, CENTER.
Assigned to Syracuse
by New York (WHA),
Kennedy helped lead the
Blazers to a Lockhart
Cup championship in
1973–1974. The center had
90 points (10th in NAHL
scoring) and 44 goals
(tied for the team lead)
in 70 games that season.
Kennedy played for New
York (WHA) in 1972–1973
and had 10 points in 54
games. His brother is NHL
veteran Forbes Kennedy.

DARRYL "SALTY" KNOWLES, RIGHT WING. Knowles (right) played in all four Blazer NAHL seasons (1973–1977), winning two championships with the team (1973–1974 and 1976–1977). He had 106 points, 44 goals, and 397 PIM in 181 games with Syracuse. Knowles skated for PHL champion San Francisco in 1977–1978. The right winger was nicknamed Salty because of his maritime background.

CARLO UGOLINI, LEFT WING. Ugolini had 57 points and 18 goals in 51 games for the 1973–1974 Lockhart Cup champion team. He had previously played three seasons for Cornell University (1970–1973), establishing several single-season and career scoring records for the Ivy League squad.

BOBBY JONES, CENTER. In 1974–1975, his only season with Syracuse, Jones led the NAHL in points (114) and led the team in assists (76). He was in the WHA for four seasons (1972–1976) with various teams, compiling 78 points and 30 goals in 161 games. He had a stint in the NHL with the Rangers in 1968–1969, and he won a Calder Cup with Buffalo (AHL) in 1969–1970.

GARRY PETERS, COACH. Peters piloted the Blazers to a Governors Cup championship in 1974–1975. He was a veteran of eight NHL seasons (1964–1972) with Montreal, the Rangers, Philadelphia, and Boston, attaining 261 PIM and 68 points in 311 games. Peters skated for two seasons in the WHA (1972–1974) with New York and Jersey. Peters was named the AHL's MVP in 1971–1972 with Boston.

THE 1973–1974 TEAM AWARDS CEREMONY. The Blazers line up with their trophies during the awards ceremony. Pictured are, from left to right, the following: Mike Smith, who was named most popular player by the Junior Booster Club; Jamie Kennedy, who was awarded the Jamie Kennedy Fan Club appreciation plaque; Mike Morton, who was given the "spirit of hockey" trophy; Butch Barber, who earned MVP and outstanding defenseman awards; Gary Sittler, who won the unsung hero award; Reg Krezanski, who was named Twin Trees Restaurant's most popular player; Coach Ron Ingram; Dave Ferguson, who received an unidentified award; and Blazer president Francis Rivette.

"THE GOALDIGGERS." Billy Goldthorpe (leaping in the air) makes the goal official with his version of the "Goldy Shuffle." Goldthorpe and Mike Morton (at the far left, in front of the goal crease) worked hard for their goals, and it is no surprise that they earned the title of "The Goaldiggers."

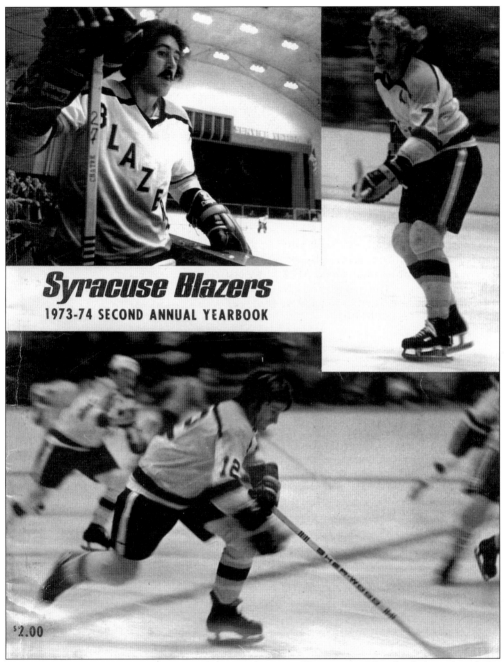

Syracuse Blazers
1973-74 SECOND ANNUAL YEARBOOK

$2.00

THE *1973–1974 SYRACUSE BLAZERS SECOND ANNUAL YEARBOOK.* This book introduced the fans to the first Blazer team of the NAHL. The full-color cover featured Claude Chartre (upper left), Lee Inglis (upper right), and Dave Ferguson (bottom). The magazine contained player profiles and photographs of current team members. The yearbook was advertised in the *Hockey News.*

SLAP SHOT. The notoriety of the NAHL and its predecessor, the EHL, were preserved for posterity in the movie *Slap Shot*, released in 1977. The film, starring Paul Newman, was based on the Johnstown Jets' NAHL championship team of 1974–1975 and its unlikely rise to the title. The screenplay was written by Nancy Dowd, sister of Jet winger Ned Dowd. The film was shot almost entirely in Johnstown, Pennsylvania, but one scene was filmed at the Onondaga War Memorial. The Hanson brothers, who stole the show, were based on the Carlson brothers, Jack, Jeff, and Steve, all actual members of the Johnstown Jets. All three were slated to act in the movie, but the Carlsons' cousin, Dave Hanson (also a Jet player), took over for Jack, who had moved up to the WHA. Ned Dowd played tough guy Ogie Ogilthorpe, based on Syracuse player Billy Goldthorpe, complete with a huge blonde Afro. Syracuse Blazers appearing in the movie included Blake Ball, Dan Belisle, Reg Krezanski, and Ray Schultz. *Slap Shot* was considered by many to be the greatest hockey movie of all time.

SEVEN

THE EAGLES
TWO TEAMS IN THE SALT CITY

Bill Charles, former Blazer owner and general manager, headed a group that purchased the American Hockey League's Jacksonville Barons and moved the team to Syracuse for the 1974–1975 season. The team had averaged less than 2,000 fans per game and suffered heavy monetary losses during its year and a half in Florida. The Barons, members of the AHL since the loop's inaugural campaign (1936–1937), had moved from Cleveland to the sunshine state in the middle of the 1972–1973 season after being driven out of town by the new Cleveland Crusaders of the World Hockey Association. The Barons had won an AHL-record nine Calder Cup championships in Cleveland.

When the Barons came to Syracuse, it had been 21 seasons since the AHL had been in town; the Syracuse Warriors last took the ice in 1953–1954. The Barons were renamed the Syracuse Eagles and shared the Onondaga War Memorial with the successful Syracuse Blazers (NAHL). The Eagles began resembling their fellow tenants; almost a dozen former Blazer players skated for the AHL team over the course of the season. Former Syracuse EHL/NAHL players included Blake Ball, Butch Barber, Dave Ferguson, Billy Goldthorpe, Gary Gresdal, Billy Orr, and Al Rycroft. Art Stratton was the Eagles' first coach, but he was replaced by John Hanna during the season.

The Eagles were affiliated with the St. Louis Blues. The AHL had a 10-team, two-division format, and Syracuse was placed in the Southern Division with Virginia, Richmond, Hershey, and Baltimore. NHL and WHA veteran Dick Sarrazin led the team in points (70) and goals (33), while NHL veteran Rich Foley led the team in assists (40). Jacques Caron played in 50 of the team's 75 games, posting a 16-21-9 record with a 3.70 GAA. The Eagles did not have much success on the ice, ending up in last place out of four teams with a 21-43-11 record and no postseason. The AHL's Southern Division was reduced to four teams during the season; the Baltimore Clippers withdrew in January 1975 when the WHA's Michigan Stags, one of the Syracuse Blazers' parent clubs, became the Baltimore Blades.

The Eagles also did not fare well in the box office, averaging only 2,349 fans per game (89,262 for 38 home dates). Syracuse fans' hockey dollars were spread thin between two minor league clubs. The AHL club's financial difficulties included back rent at the War Memorial and tax liens of almost $90,000 to the IRS. A midsummer meeting to settle the differences between the two Salt City teams failed. The Eagles turned down an offer to buy out the Blazers for $237,500.

The Eagles' future was in doubt when the club failed to show up at the annual AHL meeting. A few months later, the league printed its official schedule without including Syracuse. In mid-September, Bill Charles made an eleventh-hour pitch to the league's board of governors that he hoped would salvage the fate of the team, but the officials rejected it. The Eagles did not operate after the 1974–1975 season, ending the 39-year existence of the most successful franchise in AHL history (Cleveland/Jacksonville/Syracuse). The Blazers were the last club standing, in part because the budget to operate a team in the NAHL was much less than that needed to run an AHL team.

DICK SARRAZIN, RIGHT WING.
Sarrazin led the Eagles in scoring
(70 points) and in goals (33). Prior to
coming to Syracuse, he played with the
Philadelphia Flyers (NHL) for three
seasons (1968–1970 and 1971–1972). He
won a WHA championship with the
New England Whalers in 1972–1973.
The right winger also skated in the AHL
with Quebec (1967–1971), Richmond
(1971–1972), Jacksonville (1973–1974),
and Baltimore (1975–1976).

RICK FOLEY, DEFENSE. Foley led the Eagles
in assists (40) and PIM (306). He played in
three NHL seasons between 1970 and 1974
with Chicago, Philadelphia, and Detroit.
The defenseman played in the WHA with
Toronto in 1975–1976 and won a Patrick
Cup in 1970–1971 with Portland (WHL).

LUC SIMARD, LEFT WING. Simard scored 14 goals and registered 50 points in 74 games with the Eagles. He tallied over 60 goals in three minor league seasons: 68 goals with Cape Cod (EHL) in 1972–1973, 67 goals with Cape Cod (NAHL) in 1973–1974, and 65 goals with Beauce (NAHL) in 1975–1976. The sniper is third all-time in goals (141) and sixth all-time in points (273) in the history of the NAHL, which operated from 1973 to 1977.

MIKE CORCORAN, GOALIE. Corcoran played six games in goal for the Eagles and had a 6.31 GAA. He played junior hockey with Quebec of the Quebec Major Junior Hockey League (QMJHL) from 1972 to 1974, and he spent the 1975–1976 season in the SHL with Greensboro.

BLAKE BALL, DEFENSE. Ball played in 32 games with the Eagles and had seven assists and 86 PIM. He was one of the many former Syracuse Blazers to play for the Eagles. The former Canadian Football League veteran (1958–1964) helped Syracuse win a Walker Cup in 1972–1973. Ball accumulated 3,039 PIM in his professional hockey career (1964–1977), spending an equivalent of almost 51 games in the "sin bin."

DAVE FERGUSON, RIGHT WING. Ferguson was one of only three players to play in all 75 Eagle regular-season games. He earned 30 points and 17 goals while accumulating 117 PIM for the AHL team. The right winger also played five seasons for the Syracuse Blazers (1969–1970 and 1971–1975) and was a member of the 1972–1973 and 1973–1974 championship teams. Ferguson skated for the Cornell Big Red from 1964 to 1967.

AL RYCROFT, LEFT WING. Rycroft had 56 points and 25 goals in 70 games with the Eagles. He also played in the AHL with Jacksonville in 1973–1974. The left winger played for the Cleveland Crusaders (WHA) during part of the 1972–1973 season. He also skated in the IHL with Fort Wayne (1971–1972), the SHL with Macon (1973–1974), and the WHL with Seattle (1971–1972). Rycroft was a member of the 1972–1973 champion Blazers.

GARY GRESDAL, CENTER. Gresdal accumulated 1,712 PIM during his career in minor-league hockey, setting a new professional hockey record of 392 PIM with Jersey (EHL) in 1971–1972. Dave Schultz also had 392 PIM in the AHL that season. Gresdal racked up 162 PIM in 69 games with the Eagles. The former Blazer Walker Cup team member had a stint in the WHA with Quebec in 1975–1976.

Jean-Rene Losier, Center. Losier was second in scoring with the Eagles, earning 66 points and 28 goals during his last season of professional hockey. He had previously played in the AHL with Nova Scotia (1972–1973), the IHL with Des Moines and Fort Wayne (1969–1972), the CHL with Houston and Omaha (1968–1969 and 1973–1974), and the WHL with Denver (1969–1970).

Meehan Bonnar, Right Wing. Bonnar was the Boston Bruins' No. 1 draft pick (10th overall) in the 1967 NHL Amateur Draft, but he never made it to the NHL. He played for the Syracuse Blazers during their inaugural season (1967–1968). The right winger had 7 goals and 16 points in 40 games for the Eagles.

BILLY ORR, DEFENSE. The former Syracuse Blazer (1971–1973) had 29 points, 10 goals, and 118 PIM in 64 games with the Eagles. He was a member of Syracuse's Walker Cup team in 1972–1973. The defenseman played three other seasons in the AHL (1969–1971 and 1973–1974) with Rochester and Jacksonville, and he made it to the big leagues with Toronto (WHA) in 1973–1974.

STEVE WARR, DEFENSE. The defenseman had 28 points, 21 assists, and 109 PIM in 66 games with the Eagles. Prior to arriving in Syracuse, Warr played in the WHA with Ottawa (1972–1973) and Toronto (1973–1974). He had college hockey experience with Clarkson University (1969–1972).

CAL SWENSON, LEFT WING. Swenson played two seasons in the WHA with Winnipeg (1972–1974) prior to coming to Syracuse. He had 61 points and 27 goals in 68 games with the Eagles. The left winger played in the CHL with Tulsa from 1968 to 1972.

JOE NORIS, CENTER. Noris played parts of three NHL seasons (1971–1974) with Pittsburgh, St. Louis, and Buffalo before coming to Syracuse. He was third in Eagle scoring with 62 points and had 26 goals. The center played in the WHA from 1975 to 1978 with San Diego and Birmingham, and he was a member of the U.S. National Team in 1970–1971.

JACQUES CARON, GOALIE. Caron had a 16-21-9 record with a 3.70 GAA in 50 games for the Eagles. He played five seasons in the NHL between 1967 and 1974 with Los Angeles, St. Louis, and Vancouver. In 72 NHL games, he had a 24-29-11 record and a 3.29 GAA. The goaltender played in the WHA with Cleveland and Cincinnati from 1975 to 1977. Caron played two seasons with the Syracuse Blazers (1975–1977) and was a member of the 1976–1977 Lockhart Cup (NAHL) championship team. In 1975–1976, he was a NAHL first team all-star. The goaltender also played nine other seasons in the AHL between 1961 and 1981 with Springfield and Binghamton, and he played four seasons in the WHL with Denver (1968–1972). He was a member of Calder Cup–winning Springfield in 1961–1962 and Patrick Cup–winning Denver in 1971–1972.

EIGHT

THE FIREBIRDS
THE AHL FLIES BACK INTO TOWN

Professional hockey returned to the Salt City in 1979–1980 with the Syracuse Firebirds of the American Hockey League. The city had been without professional hockey since the Syracuse Blazers franchise was terminated after the 1976–1977 season. George Piszek, whose family operated Mrs. Paul's Kitchens, a frozen seafood company, transferred the five-year-old Philadelphia Firebirds franchise to Syracuse. The Firebirds had been losing money in the City of Brotherly Love, and club management hoped that by moving to Syracuse they could cut their financial losses and eventually create enough fan interest locally to sell the team.

The Philadelphia Firebirds were a North American Hockey League expansion team in 1974–1975. They joined the AHL in 1977–1978, shortly after the NAHL dissolved. The Firebirds, who competed against the Syracuse Blazers, had most of their success in their three NAHL seasons, earning a 123-93-6 record (.568) and winning the Lockhart Cup championship in 1975–1976. Since the Firebirds had joined the AHL, they had not attained a winning season or won a playoff round.

The AHL was a 10-team, two-division circuit in 1979–1980, and Syracuse was in the Southern Division with New York State rivals Binghamton and Rochester. The Syracuse Firebirds, who played their games at the Onondaga War Memorial, were affiliated with the Pittsburgh Penguins and the Quebec Nordiques, making them the second Syracuse franchise to have two parent clubs in the same season. Michel Parizeau was the coach of the team, but he was replaced midseason by Duane Rupp.

The Syracuse Firebirds were led by Gordie Brooks, who had been with the Firebird organization since the 1975–1976 season. Brooks, who was 10th in AHL scoring in 1979–1980, led Syracuse in all three offensive categories: points (75), goals (34), and assists (41). NHL veteran Ron Low was assigned to the Salt City sextet by Quebec and shared goaltending duties during the season. Low played in 15 games for Syracuse, earning a 5-9-1 record and a 4.64 GAA, before being called up to the parent club. Alain Cote, who also saw action in the Salt City courtesy of Quebec, was another high-profile player. Cote, who already had two WHA seasons with Quebec, went on to play in 10 NHL seasons (1979–1989) with the Nordiques. Other notable Syracuse assignees from Quebec included Gilles Bilodeau, Dave Farrish, Terry Johnson, Francois Lacombe, Terry Martin, and Pierre Plante. Pittsburgh farmhands included Jacques Cossette, Kim Davis, Jim

Hamilton, Tom Price, and Dale Tallon. The Firebirds made the playoffs with a third-place finish in their five-team division, posting a 31-42-7 record. In the postseason, Hershey swept Syracuse in four straight games during the opening round.

Despite the excitement of having professional hockey back in town after a two-year hiatus, the Firebirds drew an average of only 2,581 fans per game (103,239 for 40 home dates). The team lost just under $500,000 in 1979–1980, due largely to poor attendance. Over the summer, the team's Philadelphia-based ownership tried selling the team elsewhere; when that fell through, they attempted to move the franchise to Canada. But when St. John and then Fredericton, both in the New Brunswick province, spurned the Firebirds, Syracuse owner George Piszek decided to suspend the franchise.

A 1979–1980 FIREBIRD PROGRAM.
The Syracuse Firebirds used the same
logo that was donned by the franchise
when it was based in Philadelphia.
The logo had been the trademark of
the club since Philadelphia's inaugural
season in the NAHL in 1974–1975.

The Syracuse Firebirds $1.00
Hockey Magazine

DUANE RUPP, COACH. Rupp replaced
Michel Parizeau as Syracuse coach at
midseason. He had previously coached
Rochester (AHL) from 1976 to 1979.
As a player, he spent 10 seasons in
the NHL (1962–1963 and 1964–1973)
with the Rangers, Toronto, Minnesota,
and Pittsburgh. The defenseman was a
member of four Calder Cup–winning
teams: Springfield (1961–1962),
Rochester (1964–1965 and 1965–1966),
and Hershey (1973–1974).

91

GORDIE BROOKS, RIGHT WING. Brooks led Syracuse in points (75), goals (34), and assists (41). He played five seasons in the Firebird organization (1975–1980) and is the franchise's all-time leader in points (464), goals (223), assists (241), and games played (378). The Firebird great played three seasons in the NHL with St. Louis (1971–1972 and 1973–1974) and Washington (1974–1975), and he won a Lockhart Cup with Philadelphia (NAHL) in 1975–1976.

RON LOW, GOALIE. Low was 5-9-1 with a 4.64 GAA in 15 games with Syracuse. Low had an 11-year NHL career between 1972 and 1985 with Toronto, Washington, Detroit, Quebec, Edmonton, and New Jersey. The goaltender was 102-203-38 in the NHL with a 4.28 GAA. Low coached Edmonton (NHL) from 1994 to 1999 and the New York Rangers from 2000 to 2002, compiling an NHL coaching record of 208-248-49 (.460).

TERRY JOHNSON, DEFENSE. Johnson led Syracuse in PIM with 163. The defenseman had 13 points in 74 games in the Salt City. A veteran of nine NHL seasons (1979–1988) with Quebec, St. Louis, Calgary, and Toronto, he compiled 580 PIM and 27 points in 285 games. Johnson also played in the AHL with Hershey, Fredericton, and Newmarket.

TERRY MARTIN, FORWARD. Martin registered 18 points and 9 goals in 18 games with Syracuse. The forward had 479 games of NHL experience with Buffalo, Quebec, Toronto, Edmonton, and Minnesota, tallying 104 goals and 205 points. He won a SHL playoff championship with Charlotte in 1975–1976 and had a stint with the 1984–1985 Stanley Cup champion Edmonton Oilers.

JOHN STEWART, CENTER. Stewart was the second leading scorer on the Firebirds with 68 points. He also netted 28 goals. The center played two seasons with the Syracuse Blazers (1975–1977), winning a Lockhart Cup in 1976–1977. He also played five seasons in the WHA (1974–1979) with Cleveland and Birmingham, compiling 152 points in 271 games. The former Blazer had a stint in the NHL with Quebec in 1979–1980.

DAVE FARRISH, DEFENSE. Farrish had 14 points in 14 games with Syracuse. In seven seasons in the NHL (1976–1981 and 1982–1984) with the Rangers, Quebec, and Toronto, he had 127 points and 440 PIM in 430 games. Farrish won a Calder Cup and the AHL's outstanding defenseman award while playing with New Brunswick (AHL) in 1981–1982. The defenseman went on to coach in the AHL, IHL, and East Coast Hockey League (ECHL).

GILLES BILODEAU, LEFT WING. The winger amassed 1,916 PIM in his professional hockey career, including 451 PIM in one regular season with Beauce (NAHL) in 1975–1976. In 61 games with Syracuse, he had 131 PIM. Bilodeau spent four seasons in the WHA (1975–1979) with Toronto, Birmingham, and Quebec. He also played in the NHL with Quebec in 1979–1980.

FRANCOIS LACOMBE, DEFENSE. Lacombe notched 29 points in 50 games with the Firebirds. He played in all seven seasons of the WHA (1972–1979) with Quebec and Calgary, and he had 177 points and 139 assists in 440 games. The defenseman was a member of the 1976–1977 Avco World Trophy–winning Nordiques, and he spent four seasons in the NHL (1968–1971 and 1979–1980) with Oakland, Buffalo, and Quebec.

LOUIS SLEIGHER, RIGHT WING. In 58 games with Syracuse, Sleigher had 43 points and 28 goals. He went on to play in six NHL seasons (1979–1980 and 1981–1986) with Quebec and Boston, scoring 46 goals and 99 points in 194 games. He won a Mitchell Cup with Erie (EHL) in 1980–1981 and made it up to the WHA with Birmingham in 1978–1979.

JACQUES COSSETTE, RIGHT WING. Cossette was the only Syracuse Firebird to play in all 78 of his team's regular-season games, tallying 25 goals and 48 points. Prior to coming to Syracuse, he played three seasons in the NHL with Pittsburgh (1975–1976 and 1977–1979). Cossette was selected by Pittsburgh in round two of the 1974 NHL Amateur Draft; he was No. 27 overall.

STEVE COATES, RIGHT WING. Coates had 33 points and 10 goals in 67 games with the Firebirds. He played briefly with Detroit (NHL) in 1976–1977 and was a member of Calder Cup–winning Maine (AHL) in 1977–1978.

JIM HAMILTON, LEFT WING. Hamilton had 16 goals and 35 points in 50 games with Syracuse. He played in 95 games during eight seasons with Pittsburgh (NHL) from 1977 to 1985. His NHL totals were 32 points and 14 goals in 95 games. The left winger was selected by Pittsburgh in round two of the 1977 NHL Amateur Draft; he was No. 30 overall.

GARY CARR, GOALIE. Carr earned a 22-21-2 record and a 4.43 GAA in 45 games between the pipes for the Firebirds. The goaltender led Dayton (IHL) to a Turner Cup championship in 1975–1976. He also played in the AHL with Rochester (1976–1979), Springfield (1980–1981), and Fredericton (1981–1982).

TOM PRICE, DEFENSE. The defenseman had 38 points and 34 assists in 68 games with Syracuse. Prior to arriving in the Salt City, he spent parts of five seasons in the NHL (1974–1979) with California, Cleveland, and Pittsburgh. Price won an Adams Cup championship with Salt Lake City (CHL) in 1974–1975.

ROLAND CLOUTIER, CENTER. Cloutier was fourth on the 'Birds in scoring, earning 56 points. The center also netted 19 goals. He played 34 games over three seasons in the NHL (1977–1980) with Detroit and Quebec, totaling 17 points and 8 goals. Cloutier also played in the AHL with Nova Scotia in 1980–1981.

KIM DAVIS, CENTER. Davis had 26 points and scored 13 goals in 45 games with Syracuse. The center played parts of four NHL seasons (1977–1981) with Pittsburgh and Toronto, registering 12 points in 36 games. He won a Calder Cup in 1981–1982 with New Brunswick (AHL).

JOHN BABY, DEFENSE. The defenseman collected 27 points and 73 PIM in 73 games with Syracuse. Prior to coming to the Salt City, Baby played in two NHL seasons (1977–1979) with Cleveland and Minnesota. He also played in the AHL with Binghamton (1977–1978 and 1980–1981), the CHL with Oklahoma City (1978–1979) and Phoenix (1977–1978), and the IHL with Kalamazoo (1983–1984).

MIKE KORNEY, DEFENSE. Korney had 27 points and 87 PIM in 73 games with Syracuse. The defenseman played four seasons in the NHL (1973–1976 and 1978–1979) with Detroit and the Rangers, earning 19 points in 77 games. He won an Adams Cup with Kansas City (CHL) in 1976–1977, and he had stints with two Calder Cup–winning teams: Springfield (1974–1975) and Maine (1977–1978).

PETER MARRIN, CENTER. Marrin played in five games with Syracuse and had two points and four PIM. Marrin spent six seasons in the WHA with Toronto and Birmingham, producing 193 points and 81 goals in 277 games. The center was selected by Montreal in the second round of the 1973 NHL Amateur Draft; he was No. 22 overall.

GREG TEBBUTT, DEFENSE. Tebbutt had five points and 35 PIM in 14 games with the Firebirds. He won two Mitchell Cups with Erie (EHL) in 1979–1980 and 1980–1981. He was called up to Quebec (NHL) for two games in 1979–1980 and played part of the 1983–1984 season with Pittsburgh (NHL).

NINE

THE HORNETS
THE 10-GAME TEAM

It looked like the Salt City was going to have two professional hockey teams for the 1980–1981 season when the Eastern Hockey League granted an expansion franchise to the Syracuse Hornets. But the Syracuse Firebirds (AHL) suspended operations a few months after the announcement of the Hornets' franchise.

The new EHL was in its third season of existence and was known as the North Eastern Hockey League (NEHL) in 1978–1979, its inaugural season. The league changed its name prior to its second year to better reflect the geography of the league, which now had southern teams. The EHL, which was considered to be a lower-level minor league behind the AHL and CHL, had a six-team format for the 1980–1981 season. Teams in the EHL competed for the Mitchell Cup, named after John Mitchell, who helped organize the league and had been owner of the defunct Johnstown franchise.

The Hornets were owned by area contractor Gaetan Gagne, who had been associated with the Blazers and the Eagles. The team became the first professional hockey team since the Syracuse Stars (IAHL) to schedule all of its home games at the State Fairgrounds Coliseum, which had been recently refurbished. The major reason for being based at the Coliseum rather than the War Memorial was to save money, both for the team and the fans. The rent at the Coliseum was about one-third that of the War Memorial, and parking was free. This allowed the Hornets' management to set lower ticket and concession prices.

Former Syracuse Blazer Bill Horton was general manager and coach of the Hornets. Horton was a three-year veteran of the WHA (1972–1975) and had coaching experience as an assistant coach for Mohawk Valley (NAHL), Los Angeles (PHL), and Utica (EHL). The Hornets operated independently of any NHL affiliation and had problems obtaining quality players. Horton held a two-day open tryout camp for central New York players in addition to the regular preseason camp. He also contacted NHL clubs directly for players. The Hartford Whalers (NHL) came through and assigned goalies Bill Milner and Jay Palladino.

At the start of the season, Horton's Hornets took some sound drubbings at the hands of their opponents. After opening night, which drew 1,421 fans, crowds for the next four home games were between 700 and 800 per contest. Club management met with War Memorial officials to discuss the possibility of obtaining dates for the downtown building in an attempt to attract fans.

Hornets officials were reportedly also dissatisfied with the lack of practice time and the poorly functioning heating at the Coliseum.

Horton tried everything to make the franchise work. He kept in constant contact with major-league clubs for players and even laced up for three games. The Hornets were scheduled to play a 72-game schedule, but they suspended operations after playing only 10 games (with a 0-9-1 record) due to a lack of funds, fan interest, and adequate players to make the team competitive. The end came for the Hornets when the team failed to show up in Salem and Baltimore for regularly scheduled league games. EHL commissioner Bill Beagan gave team owner Gaetan Gagne the legal 72-hour allowance to keep the Hornets in business. The team made its last payroll, but there was some doubt that it had the funds to meet the next payroll or to carry on the day-to-day operations of the team. The Hornets only drew an average of 923 fans for five home dates (4,617 fans overall), and not all of those in attendance paid for their tickets. Horton immediately attempted to move the team to Utica for the remainder of the season, but the EHL Board of Governors decided that the transfer would be too risky and voted against it.

Former Syracuse Firebird Kevin Zappia, a native of Massena, led the team in points (14) and assists (7) and was tied with Dave Tracy for most goals (7). Some other noteworthy Hornets included Jay Leach, who became an assistant coach in the NHL and a head coach in the AHL; Paul Mancini, a fifth-round draft pick by the Los Angeles Kings; and Gary McFadyen, a third-round draft pick by the Toronto Maple Leafs, who played in the CHL and IHL.

Only two EHL cities, Baltimore and Salem, were ready to operate in the league for the following season. The loop added five new franchises, including Bill Horton's Utica-based Mohawk Valley Stars, and was renamed the Atlantic Coast Hockey League (ACHL) for the 1981–1982 season.

Jay Palladino, Goalie. Palladino came to the Hornets by way of Hartford (NHL) after having played at Salem State College. He had a horrid 9.27 GAA in six games with Syracuse. After the Hornets folded, the goaltender cut his GAA by more than half to 4.04 with Turner Cup champion Saginaw (IHL) in 1980–1981.

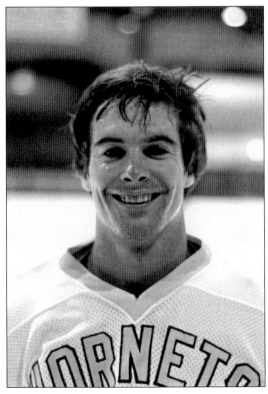

Bill Milner, Goalie. Assigned to Syracuse by the Hartford Whalers (NHL), Milner had previously had minor professional experience with Johnstown (EHL) in 1979–1980. The goaltender also played three years with Providence College (1976–1979). Milner had a whopping 10.00 GAA in eight games with the Hornets.

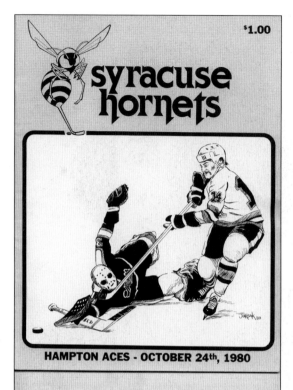

$1.00

syracuse
hornets

HAMPTON ACES - OCTOBER 24th, 1980

THE 1980–1981 HORNETS' OPENING NIGHT PROGRAM. The Hornets became the sixth team in minor-league hockey history to go winless in a season, including teams that folded midseason. The 0-9-1 Hornets were the first professional team since the 1948–1949 Windsor Ryancretes (0-25-6) of the IHL to have a winless season. No professional hockey team in North America has gone a season without a win since.

BILL HORTON, GENERAL MANAGER AND COACH. The former Syracuse Blazer returned to the Salt City as general manager and coach of the Hornets. Though the head coaching career of "Horty" got off to a slow start with Syracuse, he later guided two of his teams to ACHL championships: Mohawk Valley in 1981–1982 and Erie in 1983–1984. He was named ACHL Coach of the Year in 1981–1982. The defenseman was assigned to the Blazers by Boston (NHL) in 1967–1968.

ED WALKER, DEFENSE. Walker was a bright spot in the Hornets' "Swiss cheese" defense. He led the team with 46 PIM in nine games. The defenseman played the next two seasons in the ACHL with Mohawk Valley (1981–1983) and was a member of the 1981–1982 championship team.

ERNEST BOUTIN, CENTER. Boutin registered four points in four games with Syracuse, including two goals. He spent the rest of his professional career (1981–1984) in the ACHL, where he was a member of two Payne Trophy championship teams: Mohawk Valley (1981–1982) and Erie (1983–1984).

DICK POPIEL, DEFENSE. In seven games with the Hornets, "Pope" had six points and 24 PIM. He had previously skated in the IHL (1978–1980) with Milwaukee, Dayton, and Saginaw. The defenseman played in all six seasons of the ACHL (1981–1987) and was a member of two championship teams, Mohawk Valley (1981–1982) and Erie (1983–1984). Popiel ranks fourth all-time in games played (268) and fifth all-time in assists (215) in ACHL history.

TEN

THE CRUNCH
PROFESSIONAL HOCKEY RETURNS

Professional hockey returned to Syracuse after a 13-year absence when the Vancouver Canucks moved their American Hockey League affiliate, the Hamilton Canucks, to the Salt City in 1994–1995. The new team was called the Syracuse Crunch and was coached by Jack McIlhargey. Although the team finished last in its five-team division with a 29-42-9 record, Syracuse hockey fans came out to the War Memorial in droves; attendance totaled 235,534, an average of 5,888 fans per game.

The Crunch craze continued in 1995–1996, as season attendance grew to 237,940, an average of 5,948 fans per game. The club led the AHL in sellouts (18) during the regular season. Syracuse improved to a 31-44-5 mark and made the playoffs. It was in the "second season" that the real hysteria began. Syracuse defeated Binghamton three games to one and then ousted Baltimore in seven games in the first two playoff rounds. Syracuse faced Rochester in the semifinals but lost four games to one.

In 1996–1997, Syracuse led the AHL in sellouts again, with 11. The team averaged 5,809 fans per game and boasted a total attendance of 232,397, filling the building to a three-year league-leading 94 percent capacity. The Crunch finished fourth in their division with a 32-38-10 record. In the first round of the playoffs, Rochester swept Syracuse in three games.

Syracuse hoped to upgrade its level of talent in 1997–1998, when it became affiliated with the Pittsburgh Penguins. Having two parent clubs may have made a difference: The Crunch had their first winning season, posting a record of 35-34-11 and finishing in third place in their division. The locals lost in the opening round of the playoffs to the Hamilton Bulldogs, three games to two. Lonny Bohonos, who played on the Crunch from 1994 to 1998, left the team as the all-time leader in points (230), goals (104), and assists (126).

The Crunch did not experience much success in 1998–1999, going 18-53-9 and missing the playoffs. There was a high player turnover from the year before. Only one player cracked the 20-goal mark, and the squad let in a league-high 327 goals. It was Jack McIlhargey's last season behind the bench.

Vancouver was Syracuse's lone affiliate for the 1999–2000 season. New coach Stan Smyl guided the team to a second-place finish in their division with a 35-36-9 record. Forward Harold

Druken was named to the AHL's all-rookie team. The Salt City sextet was eliminated in the first round of the playoffs, losing to Hamilton three games to one.

The Crunch became the top farm team of the NHL expansion Columbus Blue Jackets in 2000–2001. Syracuse finished in third place in their division, going 33-35-12 and earning a playoff berth behind new coach Gary Agnew. Bill Bowler became the first Crunch player to place in the AHL's top 10 in scoring, ranking sixth with 79 points. Defensemen Mike Gaul and Radim Bicanek became the first Crunch players to be named to the AHL's all-star team, both as second team selections. Syracuse faced Wilkes-Barre/Scranton in the opening playoff round and lost three games to two.

The Crunch had their most successful season during the 2001–2002 campaign, winning their first division title and regular-season conference championship. In the process, team records were set for regular-season wins (39) and points in the standings (96). In the postseason, Syracuse swept Philadelphia in a first-round best-of-five series but lost in the next round to Chicago in seven games. The club finished with a 39-28-13 record for its second winning season in franchise history. Second team all-star Jean-Francois Labbe rewrote the Crunch record book, including team records for GAA (2.18) and shutouts (nine).

In 2002–2003, a lack of firepower on offense—only one team member broke the 20-goal or 50-point barriers—contributed to a 27-45-8 record and no postseason. Columbus assigned Pascal Leclaire, their No. 1 draft pick (No. 8 overall) in the 2001 NHL Entry Draft, to Syracuse. Leclaire appeared in 36 games and had a 3.56 GAA.

The Crunch celebrated their 10th anniversary during the 2003–2004 season. Syracuse barely missed capturing its second division title, finishing in second place with a 38-32-10 record. Donald MacLean was among the AHL's top-10 scorers, placing eighth with 69 points. In the playoffs, the locals battled Rochester to a seven-game opening round thriller, but they came up short.

The 2004–2005 season was a record-breaking year for Crunch fan favorite Brad Moran. Moran, who played for Syracuse from 2000 to 2005, established new all-time team records for points (241), assists (143), power-play goals (38), and games played (334). It was also a milestone season for the Crunch franchise as the club became the first Salt City professional hockey team to play in 11 seasons (1994–2005). Syracuse narrowly missed the playoffs with a 36-44 record and a fifth-place finish in their division.

BRAD MORAN, CENTER. During the 2004–2005 season, the center established new all-time, regular-season team records for points (241), assists (143), power-play goals (38), and games played (334). He also holds the team's all-time record for shorthanded goals (nine). Moran is only seven tallies away from breaking the all-time Crunch record for goals, and he is two game-winning goals away from shattering the team's all-time record in that category. In 2001–2002, he led the team in goals (25), and in 2004–2005, he led the team in points (72) and assists (46). The center had brief call ups to Columbus (NHL) during the 2001–2002 and 2003–2004 seasons. Moran played five seasons with Calgary (1995–2000) in the WHL, including the President's Cup championship team of 1998–1999, collecting 450 points and 204 goals in 357 games.

MARK WOTTON, DEFENSE. Wotton is third all-time in points (164), assists (124), and games played (310) for the Crunch. The defenseman skated for five seasons with Syracuse (1994–1999), leading the team in assists (31) in 1998–1999. Wotton played parts of four NHL seasons (between 1994 and 2001) with Vancouver and Dallas. He had nine points and 25 PIM in 43 NHL games.

JACK McILHARGEY, COACH. McIlhargey coached the Crunch for five seasons (1994–1999), compiling a 145-211-44 record (.418). He led Syracuse to the postseason three times, including a semifinals appearance in 1995–1996. After coaching in the Salt City, he became an assistant coach with Vancouver (NHL) from 1999 to 2003. McIlhargey played eight seasons in the NHL (1974–1982) and racked up 1,102 PIM in 393 games.

MIKE PECA, CENTER. Peca played in the Crunch's inaugural season (1994–1995), earning 34 points and 10 goals in 35 games. A veteran of 10 NHL seasons (1993–2000 and 2001–2004), he compiled 371 points and 151 goals in 622 games. Peca is a two-time winner of the Frank J. Selke Trophy for best defensive forward in the NHL (1996–1997 and 2001–2002).

REGGIE SAVAGE, RIGHT WING. Savage is second all-time in power-play goals (36) and third all-time in goals (82) in Crunch history. He garnered 145 points and 63 assists in three seasons with Syracuse (1995–1996 and 1999–2001). Savage led the Crunch in goals scored during 1999–2000 (36) and 2000–2001 (37). He also holds the team record for power-play goals in a season (20), set in 2000–2001.

REG SAVAGE

LONNY BOHONOS, CENTER. Bohonos ranks high on several all-time Crunch lists: He is first in goals (104), second in points (230), second in assists (126), and tied for first in game-winning goals (14). He played four seasons with the Crunch (1994–1998) and left the team as the all-time leader in points and assists. Bohonos holds the Crunch single-season record for goals (40) and is tied for the most points in a season (79); both records were set in 1995–1996. He also led the team in goals in 1996–1997 with 22 and in assists in 1994–1995 and 1995–1996 with 45 and 39, respectively. Bohonos set single-game Crunch records for points (six) and assists (six) during the 1995–1996 season. The fan favorite had stints in the NHL with Vancouver (1995–1998) and Toronto (1997–1999), recording 35 points and 19 goals in 83 games.

DANA MURZYN, DEFENSE. Murzyn played in more NHL regular-season games (838) than any other Crunch player. The defenseman had 14 years of NHL experience (1985–1999) with Hartford, Calgary, and Vancouver, collecting 1571 PIM and 205 points. He won a Stanley Cup with Calgary in 1988–1989. Murzyn had 37 PIM and six points in 20 games with the Crunch (1998–1999).

DAN KESA, RIGHT WING. In the Crunch's inaugural season (1994–1995), Kesa led the team in points (78) and goals (34). He played in 139 NHL games with Vancouver, Dallas, Pittsburgh, and Tampa Bay between 1993 and 2000, earning 30 points and 22 assists. He won a Turner Cup with Detroit (IHL) in 1996–1997.

BRIAN LONEY, RIGHT WING. Loney shares the team record for most game-winning goals in a season with seven, a record set in 1995–1996. He is also tied for the most Crunch game-winning goals of all time with 14. From 1994 to 1997, Loney compiled 149 points, 76 goals, and 378 PIM in 191 games with Syracuse. He led the Crunch in points (58) and assists (39) in 1996–1997. In 1995–1996, Loney played with the Canucks (NHL).

LARRY COURVILLE, LEFT WING. Courville played four seasons with Syracuse (1995–1999), compiling 152 points, 56 goals, and 469 PIM in 225 games. He was selected by Vancouver in round three of the 1995 NHL Entry Draft; he was No. 61 overall. The left winger had three stints in the NHL with the Canucks (1995–1998), earning three points and 16 PIM in 33 games.

TRENT KLATT, RIGHT WING. Klatt appeared in the second-highest number of NHL regular-season games (781) of any Crunch player. In his 13 NHL seasons (1991–2004), Klatt had 343 points, 143 goals, and 307 PIM with Minnesota, Dallas, Philadelphia, Vancouver, and Los Angeles. In his only season with Syracuse (1999–2000), he had 23 points and 13 goals in 24 games.

TYSON NASH, LEFT WING. In three seasons with Syracuse (1995–1998), Nash had 347 PIM and 85 points in 201 games. An NHL veteran of six years (1998–2004) with St. Louis and Phoenix, Nash had 589 PIM and 58 points in 324 games. He won three President's Cups in the WHL (1991–1992, 1993–1994, and 1994–1995) during his five seasons with Kamloops (1990–1995).

ZENITH KOMARNISKI, DEFENSE. In his four seasons in the Salt City (1998–2000 and 2003–2005), Komarniski compiled 82 points and 402 PIM in 216 games. The defenseman was in the NHL with Vancouver and Columbus for parts of three seasons between 1999 and 2004, appearing in 21 games. Vancouver selected him in the third round of the 1996 NHL Entry Draft; he was No. 75 overall.

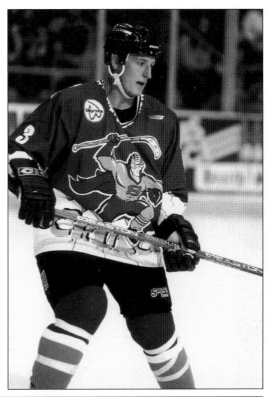

SCOTT WALKER, RIGHT WING. Walker tied for the most PIM (334) on the Crunch during 1994–1995, sharing a team record at the time. The right winger played part of the 1995–1996 season with Syracuse before finding a niche in the NHL, where he stayed for the next eight seasons. Walker had 895 PIM, 275 points, and 101 goals in 574 games during his 10 NHL seasons (1994–2004) with Vancouver and Nashville.

ALL-STARS IN THE SALT CITY.
The Salt City was selected to host the AHL's All-Star Game and All-Star Skills Competition. The game was played on February 11, 1998. Canada beat PlanetUSA (composed of players from the United States and Europe) 11-10 in front of a sellout crowd of 6,230 at the War Memorial. The game was broadcast to over 65 million households on live television across the United States on ESPN2, throughout Canada on TSN and RDS, and in Mexico and the Caribbean on ESPN-dos. Eleven records were broken in the game, including most goals in a game and in a period, fastest three goals by one team and by both teams, and most shots in a game by one team and by both teams. The All-Star Skills Competition, played the day before, was also a huge success.

THE 1998–1999 CRUNCH FIFTH ANNIVERSARY PROGRAM. In 1998–1999, the Crunch became the only Syracuse-based AHL team to celebrate its fifth anniversary. The four previous Syracuse AHL teams—the Stars, Warriors, Eagles, and Firebirds—never made it to their fifth AHL season. The Crunch have played more AHL seasons in Syracuse than the other four Salt City AHL franchises combined.

JOHN BADDUKE, RIGHT WING. Badduke is the only Crunch player to have his uniform number (No. 14) retired. Badduke's 649 PIM in 114 games from 1994 to 1997 ranks second all-time for Syracuse. He tied for the most PIM on the team in 1994–1995 with 334, a team record at the time. The right winger accumulated 3,029 PIM in his professional and major junior hockey careers.

JEAN-FRANCOIS LABBE, GOALIE. Labbe is the all-time Crunch leader in GAA (2.48) and shutouts (11). In 2001–2002, he set all-time franchise single-season marks for lowest GAA (2.18) and save percentage (92.8 percent). He also set the team single-season record for shutouts with nine, tying a 59-year-old AHL record in the process. Labbe was the first Crunch goalie to earn back-to-back shutouts and had a 43-33-13 record in his three seasons with Syracuse (2000–2003). He is 6th all-time in the AHL in shutouts (27) and 10th all-time in the AHL in wins (202). He won two Calder Cups, one with Hershey in 1996–1997 and one with Hartford in 1999–2000. While playing for Hershey in 1996–1997, Labbe took home the AHL's MVP award, the outstanding goaltender award, and the award for lowest GAA (which he also shared in 1999–2000 while playing with Hartford). The record holder had stints in the NHL with the Rangers (1999–2000) and Columbus (2001–2003). In the Colonial Hockey League (CoHL), Labbe led Thunder Bay to a Colonial Cup championship in 1993–1994, and he also won the best goaltender, rookie of the year, and playoff MVP awards.

JODY SHELLEY, LEFT WING. Shelley set the Crunch's all-time, single-season record for penalty minutes with 357 in 2000–2001. He played two seasons for Syracuse (2000–2002) before securing a permanent home in the Blue Jackets' (NHL) lineup. The left winger piled up 693 PIM in 197 NHL games with Columbus (2000–2004).

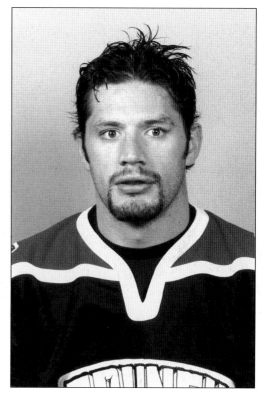

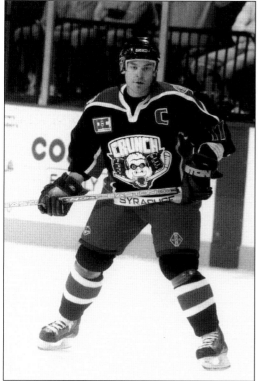

DAVID LING, RIGHT WING. Ling played three seasons with the Crunch (2001–2004), compiling 118 points, 33 goals, and 394 PIM in 131 games. The winger led Syracuse in assists in 2001–2002 with 41 and in 2002–2003 with 34. In 2001–2002, he led the team in PIM with 240. Ling had experience in the NHL with Montreal (1996–1998) and Columbus (2001–2004), earning 191 PIM and eight points in 93 games.

MIKE PANDOLFO, LEFT WING. Pandolfo registered 71 points, 35 goals, and 78 PIM in 213 games during three seasons with the Crunch (2002–2005). He played three games with Columbus (NHL) in 2003–2004. From 1998 to 2002, the winger skated for Boston University. Buffalo selected him in round three of the 1998 NHL Entry Draft; he was No. 77 overall.

MATHIEU DARCHE, LEFT WING. In three seasons with Syracuse (2000–2003), Darche had 149 points and 70 goals in 205 games. He led the Crunch in scoring (64 points) and goals (32) during the 2002–2003 season. The winger was called up to Columbus (NHL) during all three of his seasons with Syracuse, appearing in 24 games for the Blue Jackets. He won a Calder Cup in 2003–2004 with Milwaukee (AHL).

TYLER SLOAN, DEFENSE. A veteran of four Syracuse seasons (2001–2005), Sloan had 11 points and 119 PIM in 124 games. Prior to coming to the Salt City, the defenseman skated for Kamloops (WHL) for two seasons (2000–2002). He also spent time in the ECHL with Dayton (2002–2003 and 2004–2005).

MATT DAVIDSON, RIGHT WING. Davidson had 79 points and 41 goals in 167 games during three campaigns with Syracuse (2000–2003). He shares the team record for short-handed goals in a season with four in 2002–2003. The right winger skated for the parent Blue Jackets (NHL) in each of his seasons with the Crunch, registering 12 points and 5 goals in 56 games.

DARREL SCOVILLE, DEFENSE. Scoville had 76 points and 159 PIM in 145 games during three seasons with Syracuse (2001–2004). He had three stints in the NHL between 1999 and 2004 with Calgary and Columbus, and he won a Calder Cup with St. John (AHL) in 2000–2001.

MIKE FOUNTAIN, GOALIE. Fountain is second all-time between the pipes in wins (54) and games played (140) for the Crunch. He had a 3.59 GAA in his three seasons with Syracuse (1994–1997). The goaltender had four stints in the NHL between 1996 and 2001 with Vancouver, Carolina, and Ottawa, earning a 3.48 GAA in 11 games. He was a member of the Canadian National Team in 1992–1993.

JEREMY REICH, LEFT WING. Reich is the Crunch's all-time penalty minute king. He accumulated 820 PIM over five seasons (2000–2005), including a team season high of 195 PIM in 2002–2003. Reich also had 118 points and 71 assists in 315 games with Syracuse. He got the call to Columbus (NHL) for nine games in 2003–2004. The "bad boy" played in the WHL with Seattle and Swift Current from 1995 to 2000.

SEAN PRONGER, CENTER. Pronger spent two seasons in Syracuse (2001–2002 and 2003–2004). In 61 games in the Salt City, he had 51 points, 25 goals, and 60 PIM. A journeyman of seven teams over eight seasons in the NHL (1995–2000 and 2001–2004), the center had 59 points, 23 goals, and 159 PIM in 260 games. He is the brother of NHL veteran Chris Pronger.

TIM JACKMAN, RIGHT WING. Jackman was selected by Columbus in round two (No. 38 overall) of the 2001 NHL Entry Draft. He had 87 points, 46 goals, and 207 PIM in 214 games with Syracuse (2002–2005). The winger was up with Columbus (NHL) for 19 games in 2003–2004 and had three points and 16 PIM.

KARL GOEHRING, GOALIE. Goehring was between the pipes in more games (151) than any other Crunch goaltender. He also holds the all-time Crunch record for wins (63) and is second all-time in shutouts (9) and GAA (2.66). Goehring played four seasons in the Salt City (2001–2005).

A 2000–2001 Crunch Program. The Crunch unveiled a new logo and sported new colors for the 2000–2001 season to commemorate their new affiliation with the Columbus Blue Jackets. Syracuse was believed to be the first professional hockey team in North America to use a gorilla as its logo. The club's new colors were red, white, and blue to mirror its Columbus (NHL) parent club.

CRUNCH TIMES

VOLUME 4 ISSUE 1

Crunch Hockey:
IT'S GORILLA WARFARE

Gary Agnew, Coach. Agnew piloted the Crunch for five seasons (2000–2005) and compiled a 173-184-43 record while leading the team to three playoff appearances. He guided the team to its most successful season in 2001–2002, winning a division title and a regular-season conference title while establishing team records for regular-season wins (39) and points in the standings (96).

THE 10TH ANNIVERSARY LOGO. The Crunch announced their 10th Anniversary All-Time Team, as voted by the fans, during the 2003–2004 season. The first team was made up of the following: Gary Agnew, coach; J. F. Labbe, goalie; Derrick Walser, defense; Brent Sopel, defense; Lonny Bohonos, right wing; Reggie Savage, left wing; and Sean Pronger, center. The second team consisted of the following: Jack McIlhargey, coach; Karl Goehring, goalie; Adrian Aucoin, defense; Duvie Westcott, defense; David Ling, right wing; Mathieu Darche, left wing; and Mike Peca, center. The fans also voted on the Crunch's greatest tough guy of all time, greatest team of all time, and greatest moment of all time. The greatest tough guy award went to Jody Shelley, and the greatest team was the 2001–2002 Crunch. The greatest moment was David Ling's last-second game-tying goal and then his game-winning overtime goal versus Albany on April 6, 2002, which gave Syracuse its first-ever regular-season conference championship.